Paola Leopizzi Harris

EXOPOLITICS

How Does One Speak To A Ball Of Light?

Protocols For Future Contact

Interviews With Top Level Witnesses

Bloomington, IN  Milton Keynes, UK

authorHOUSE®

AuthorHouse™
1663 Liberty Drive, Suite 200
Bloomington, IN 47403
www.authorhouse.com
Phone: 1-800-839-8640

AuthorHouse™ UK Ltd.
500 Avebury Boulevard
Central Milton Keynes, MK9 2BE
www.authorhouse.co.uk
Phone: 08001974150

This book is a work of non-fiction. Unless otherwise noted, the author and the publisher make no explicit guarantees as to the accuracy of the information contained in this book and in some cases, names of people and places have been altered to protect their privacy.

First published by AuthorHouse 4/11/2007

ISBN: 978-1-4259-9402-0 (sc)

Library of Congress Control Number: 2007900739

Printed in the United States of America
Bloomington, Indiana

This book is printed on acid-free paper.

Paola Leopizzi Harris
Cover design by Alberto Forgione
Contributions and ideas: Fran Pickering (UK)
Lucie Blanchard (USA)
Photographs@ Paola Harris 2006

This book is dedicated to all those who are working towards
full disclosure.
Alberto, Paolo, Adriano Forgione, Pino Morelli and all
those in Hera Edizioni; Italy
In particular Area 51 magazine editor Maurizio Baiata
Translators Lavinia Pallotta, Teresa Barbatelli and Dawn
Bissell, whose vision and dedication have no bounds,
Webmasters Giovanni Zavarelli and Alejandro Rojas
Also all those, who in this book, chose to
reveal the truth about the extraterrestrial presence on Earth.

You are the courageous ones.

Endorsements

Paola Harris has succeeded brilliantly in exposing the truth about the extraterrestrial presence and how that may affect our lives and future relationships. Reading Paola's work will open your eyes to the reality of what you have only dared to imagine.

Honorable Paul Hellyer, former Minister of National Defence, Canada.

My friend, International journalist researcher, Paola Harris believes that "we are not alone in the Universe" and that we have hope for the evolution of mankind into a peaceful, cooperative species worthy of joining other civilizations in exploring "inner" as well as "outer" space!

Uri Geller.

She has been my dedicated friend and "Guardian Angel" for about six years, since we toured the Kennedy Space Center in 2000. Although Paola is relatively new to the UFO scene, she has made a large impact among many veterans, including myself, with 59 years in the field. Paola has the ears and eyes for UFO news. She is a proven photo-news journalist and can sense an interesting story any place on earth. I am proud to call her my friend.

Clark C. McClelland, *former ScO, Space Shuttle Fleet*, Kennedy Space Center, Florida, 1958 to 1992.

I first met Paola some ten years ago and, since that, we have been together many other times in conferences all over the world. She always impresses me with the amount of energy she puts into the UFO research and the Exopolitics debate and I am overwhelmed to see the many impressive results she gets from doing so. Paola has been giving a remarkable contribution to the understanding of the UFO Phenomena worldwide and should be congratulated for that. She has also been exceptionally generous in sharing her findings with other UFO researchers. The Brazilian Ufology is one among many that is in debt to Paola Harris for all her contributions.

A.J. Gevaerd, *Brazil UFO Magazine*

Beyond the dedication to journalism and beyond the deep commitment to uncover the truth of our involvement with extraterrestrial intelligence, I have always been impressed by Paola's intuitive understanding of the spiritual component in the matter. "They" who have been with us since the beginning of human history cannot be understood without addressing an intimate interrelationship that involves our human spiritual identity. Paola has always sensed that connection and conducts her research with that in mind. I admire and respect Paola's work and will always support her journalistic approach.

Sgt. Major Robert O Dean

Paola Harris has her finger on the pulse of where Ufology has been and where it needs to go. Her "big picture" perspective on the phenomenon and its researchers brings a new dimension to the field. On top of all that, she does the work that few in Ufology can or will do: bridging the gap between American Ufology and its international counterparts.

Tim Binnall, host of Binnall of America paranormal pod cast,
binnallofamerica.com

Paola is an exemplary, first-on-the-scene, globe-hopping trailblazer, in pursuit of Alien/ET Disclosure, using Exopolitical agendas and tools and getting the message out. An investigative journalist with all the no-nonsense interview techniques – and don't look her in the eye if you're not telling the truth! Nobody does it better!

'Sweeps' Fox, Ireland; Irish Ufology

Paola Harris is enlightening lightning; she arrives on the scene of both UFOs and Exopolitics like a bolt from above: high-charged, brilliant and luminous. I think the spheres of light have been communicating with Paola for a long, long time and she wants to communicate back to those spheres as a courtesy and a welcome. With Paola as their friend, those illustrious spheres from beyond will feel right at home on our planet -- and YOU will feel right at home taking Paola's well-honed wisdom about life, reality and mankind's place in the universe into your mind and your heart.

Paul Davids, *Star Wars book writer and Executive Producer of Roswell,* the Showtime film starring Kyle MacLachlan, Martin Sheen and Dwight Yoakam

In my 31 years of pursuing the truth about UFOs I have met very few people of the caliber of Paola. It was a distinct honor and pleasure to finally meet and get to know her better at X-Conferences I & II. What brought us close together quickly was our shared respect and admiration for the work of Dr. John Mack. In her life-long quest for exopolitical truth and planetary peace, there is no finer journalistic example of honesty, integrity, compassion and courage than Paola.

Mike Bird, *Director Exopolitics*, Toronto.

We will never fail to support Paola, who is the real driving force of Italian Ufology, the free and independent Ufology of this country where, in order to survive, at times you have to compromise your integrity, as researcher and journalist. We have done some amazing work together, of which our dear friend Colonel Philip Corso would be proud.

Maurizio Baiata, Editor *Area 51 Magazine* Italy

I have known Paola now since we met in Roswell, in 1997, and have watched her dogged determination to pursue the facts of the many stories of the extraterrestrial presence on earth. In addition, she has continued this pursuit on an international stage and has been connecting all the dots, and the outlines of the big picture are beginning to emerge.

Bill Hamilton, Author of *The Phoenix Lights Mystery and Project Aquarius*

Paola Harris is an investigative journalist whose quest for the truth about UFOs has taken her all around the world. Her dedication is legendary and she has obtained numerous scoops through her meticulous research and tenacious approach. Paola has made a major contribution to this subject by placing into the public domain a vast body of direct testimony from key figures in this field.

Nick Pope, UFO Researcher, UK

"Paola Harris is an Exopolitics scholar who knows first hand the facts of contact and liaison between Off-Planet Cultures and our governments. Her book *Exopolitics: How Does One Speak to a Ball of Light* is a bridge to a positive human future. It is filled with the qualities that Paola embodies as a courageous human being: Insight, Spirit, Excitement, Life, and above all Truth. Read her book and "Prosper!"

Alfred Lambremont Webre, JD, MEd – Exopolitics.com; Institute for Cooperation in Space (ICIS) and author of *Exopolitics: Politics, Government and Law in the Universe.*

Exopolitics originally emerged as a defined concept in the United States in 2000. It has since spread around the world and no one has done more to bring exopolitics to Europe than Paola Harris. Her work is now acknowledged worldwide. Through research, conferences, articles and interviews, she is helping to educate people about the most profound issue in human history – the formal disclosure of, and eventual open contact with, an extraterrestrial presence engaging the planet Earth and the human race.

Stephen Bassett, *Paradigm Research Group*

Contents

Preface: Exopolitical Challenges and Protocols for Future
    Contact   xiii
    Dr. Michael Salla

Foreword: Liaison between Off-planet Cultures and Our
    Governments   xviii
    Pascal Riolo

Essays: Taking Ufology Out of the Dark Ages   xx

        Exobiology and Exopolitics   xxiii

Section One
Unconventional Wisdom from Unconventional People

Interview: Honorable Paul Hellyer, Former Canadian Defence
    Minister   2

The Death of the Fourth Estate: Interview with Dr. Steven Greer 15

An Exopolitical Consideration and a Challenge for Researchers 19

Testimony on Bentwaters UFO Case by Steven Robert LaPlume 22

The Hynek Method: Laugh, Laugh, Study, Study   23

Interview: Betsy McDonald, Wife of Dr. James McDonald   33

Interview: Dr. Edgar Mitchell, Apollo 14 Astronaut   41

Interview: Colonel Philip Corso   50

Monsignor Corrado Balducci, Vatican Representative   53

Interview: Clark McClelland, Former ScO KSC, Regarding His
    Conversation with Senator Barry Goldwater   56

Section Two
Challenges and Protocols for Future Contact
& The Role of Galactic Diplomacy

The Philadelphia Experiment: Interview with Al Bielek   93

Protocol One: The Need to Study Exopolitics   107

The Discipline of Exopolitics   107

Protocol Two: Our Stuff or Their Stuff?   116

Protocol Three: Visitors from the Future and Dimensional Gates   122

J-Rod and Looking Glass Technology: Interview with Dr. Dan Burisch   125

Protocol Four: Viruses and Biological Contamination   135

The Varginha Case: Briefing by AJ Gevaerd Brazil   136

Protocol Five: Communication with Alien Races   148

The *Tall Whites* on Nellis Base: Interview with Charles Hall   149

The Billy Meier Case   159

Interview: "Kewanee" Jack Lapserritis. M.S., Author of *The Psychic Sasquatch and their Et Connection*   161

28 April 2005: Mysterious humanoid seen In Campania region near Naples   167

Protocol Six: Record, Collect, and Decipher the Cosmic Messages   170

The Messages From Contact: Interview with Yvonne Smith, Psychotherapist   172

Aliens living among us: Interview with Helen Littrell, Author of *Raechel's Eyes*   176

The Jason Andrews Case; *Indigo Children*   181

Protocol Seven: International Cooperation and Research Criteria   185

Travis Walton Speaks   185

Serpo and *Exempt from Disclosure* Enter the UFO Culture   187

Protocol Eight: Orbs, Spheres, and Intra-dimensional Beings   **191**

Dr. Lynne Kitei and *The Phoenix Lights* Documentary   191

BOL – Ball Of Light Phenomena in Italy, by Adriano Forgione   193

Protocol Nine: Galactic Diplomacy and Cseti Protocols   **194**

Ambassadors to the Universe Program: Interview with Dr. Steven Greer   196

Essays by Paola Leopizzi Harris: Let's Change the Prime Directive – "The Agony and the Ecstasy of Ufology: The Emergence of Exopolitics and Galactic Diplomacy as Academic Disciplines."   203

Possible Solutions   **210**

Interview: Dr. John Mack   210

So How Does One Speak to a *Ball Of Light*? Alien Communication; Light Spheres, Kyle XY, and Psychics   218

The Hawaii Declaration   223

Author Biography   226

Appendix and Bibliography   228

Exopolitical Challenges and Protocols for Future Contact

Preface by Dr. Michael Salla

Exopolitics is a revolutionary new approach to evidence concerning an extraterrestrial presence that is kept secret by a shadowy group of covert quasi-governmental organizations in the United States and other major countries. Exopolitics differs from more traditional approaches in Ufology, which focus on finding sufficient empirical evidence to indubitably prove the UFO phenomenon to be real. In contrast, exopolitics focuses on the implications of the available evidence confirming the presence of extraterrestrial visitors to our planet. Exopolitics focuses on key policy questions such as: Are extraterrestrials friends or foes? Should space weapons be targeted towards extraterrestrial visitors? What diplomatic protocols should be used for establishing contact with extraterrestrials? Finally, exopolitics focuses on identifying the key political players, institutions and processes influencing the available evidence of visitation by extraterrestrial civilizations.

The exopolitical challenge necessitates going beyond the simplistic demand for indubitable empirical evidence, and requires analysis both of how evidence is collected and analyzed and its implications. This typically leads to the realization that evidence is systematically distorted, removed or fabricated by shadowy quasi-governmental organizations intent on maintaining the "Cosmic Watergate." Exopolitics, therefore, requires an open mind and systematic attempts to investigate the best available evidence that extraterrestrials are visiting our planet, that quasi-government organizations are keeping this secret, and that the available evidence has important implications for all life on this planet. This book by Paola Harris, a veteran UFO investigative journalist, both defines the exopolitical challenges before us, and outlines some strategies for meeting these challenges.

Paola began her UFO research under the expert guidance of Dr. Allen Hynek, who began advising her in the 1970s on the importance of thoroughly investigating UFO evidence. Working under Dr. Hynek, Paola began personally investigating key UFO cases by traveling to interview witnesses and see at first hand any available evidence. She has since compiled an impressive database of witnesses and evidence confirming the reality of the UFO phenomenon and of a high-level cover-up up by quasi-governmental organizations. Her research confirms that these shadowy organizations, in the United States, use their authority and executive orders passed by a number of presidents in order to co-opt the resources and personnel of various governmental, military and corporate entities.

In her first book, *Connecting the Dots* (Wild Flower Press, 2005), Paola provided an impressive compilation of interviews with whistle-blowers and veteran UFO researchers, detailing how the UFO cover-up is organized and how suppression of the evidence occurs. Her book helped open up some of the key challenges confronting the emerging field of exopolitics. In this book, Paola explicitly addresses a number of exopolitical challenges. As her book title suggests, these include establishing reliable forms of communication with advanced non-terrestrial life forms, establishing protocols for extraterrestrial contact and finally, understanding the covert quasi-governmental cover-up.

Paola's is the latest in a series of published books that explicitly examine exopolitics and help define exopolitics as a new field of scholarly study. My own book, *Exopolitics: Political Implications of the Extraterrestrial Presence* (Dandelion Books, 2004), describes the evolution of the global management system for extraterrestrial affairs, outlines how exopolitics impacts upon conventional international politics and gives an exopolitical analysis of the Iraq war. This was followed by Alfred Webre's *Exopolitics: Politics, Government, and Law in the Universe* (Filament Books, 2005) that examines how quarantine has been imposed upon the Earth due to historically violent human policies, and what this suggests about political processes existing in "universe society."

In the essays of her new book, Paola outlines the emerging field of exopolitics and how it differs from more traditional UFO approaches. She advocates the need to break free of the myopic focus on finding indubitable empirical evidence and documentation and, instead, begin examining the implications of the available evidence, put forward by a number of credible witnesses and whistleblowers, that extraterrestrial visitation is very real. Paola correctly identifies that traditional UFO approaches are often a thinly-veiled form of debunking that systematically casts aside valuable testimonies from whistleblowers and witnesses courageously revealing the truth about extraterrestrial visitation. Having worked directly with key whistleblowers, such as the late Lt. Col. Philip Corso, she knew, all too well, the difficulty of substantiating the testimonies of those revealing the deep secrets hidden by quasi-governmental organizations behind the Cosmic Watergate. Her Essays section correctly lays out the need to study the implications of whistleblower testimonies, and the folly in thinly-veiled debunking efforts that will doom traditional Ufology to irrelevancy as the population awakens to the truth of the extraterrestrial presence.

In the subsequent *Unconventional Wisdom from Unconventional People* section of her book, she interviews some of the key people contributing to the exopolitical awakening. Most significant are the revelations from Dr. Steven Greer, former astronaut Dr. Edgar Mitchell, the Honorable Paul Hellyer and Ambassador John McDonnell, who all provide unique perspectives into the exopolitical challenges before us. Dr. Greer discusses how quasi-governmental organizations have usurped constitutional principles in maintaining the Cosmic Watergate. Dr. Mitchell reveals his own experiences, based on conversations with reliable 'insiders' that extraterrestrials are visiting Earth and government suppression of this information is very real. A former Canadian Defence Minister, Paul Hellyer, discusses the policy issues raised by US efforts to put weaponry into space and the possible targeting of extra-terrestrial visitors

The next section of Paola's book contains a number of interviews of individuals who point out the main exopolitical challenge before us in terms of developing the right protocols for extraterrestrial contact. The Charles Hall interview describes the need for developing the right protocols for interacting with extraterrestrial visitors. Hall warns that misunderstanding these protocols can have harmful consequences, as he directly experienced himself. This substantiates the need to carefully assess the development and use of advanced weaponry that might be used against extraterrestrial visitors. Another interview involves (Dr.) Dan Burisch, who describes the compartmentalized security processes used for managing human response to extraterrestrial contacts and for restricting this information. The interview with Philip Corso outlines the challenges for establishing a new world, based on human-extraterrestrial contact.

Paola finally examines, in her last section of the book, some of the protocols that might be used for establishing contact with extraterrestrial civilizations. These protocols correctly point to one of the central challenges of exopolitics: how do we communicate and act when in contact with advanced, non-terrestrial life forms? Each set of protocols point to a set of procedures that either have been used, or can be used when extraterrestrial contact occurs, in order to minimize undesirable actions and misunderstandings. Some protocols for encouraging peaceful extraterrestrial contact were agreed upon at the Extraterrestrial Civilizations and World Peace Conference in Hawaii in June, 2006. The Hawaii Declaration on Peaceful Relations with Extraterrestrial Civilizations was adopted by consensus at the conference, which comprised seventeen speakers and a total audience of almost 150. Speakers included the Honorable Paul Hellyer, Ambassador John McDonnell, Paola, Alfred Webre, Philip Corso, Jr. and I. The Declaration outlines seven key principles for promoting peaceful relations with extraterrestrial civilizations. It therefore represents an important citizen diplomacy initiative for establishing the protocols for contact with extraterrestrial civilizations. The Declaration is available online at: www.etworldpeace. com.

Paola's book is a valuable tool for all those seeking to understand how to establish formal protocols for communicating and contacting extraterrestrial civilizations. Her book makes a significant contribution to the field of exopolitics by correctly identifying the implications of the testimony provided by a number of credible witnesses and whistleblowers concerning the extraterrestrial presence. Exopolitics is an emerging field that promises to awaken many to the implications of an extraterrestrial presence that has yet to be officially acknowledged to the general public, elected political officials or the mass media. Paola Harris' book makes a great contribution to awakening many to the implications of the extraterrestrial presence. I strongly recommend it as a valuable tool for both established researchers and those just beginning their journey in understanding the exopolitical challenges confronting humanity.

Michael E. Salla, MA., PhD.
President and Founder Exopolitics Institute.
17 November 2006.
www.exopoliticsinstitute.org

Liaison between Off-planet Cultures and Our Governments

Foreword By Pascal Riolo

It all started in October 2001, when I went to St Marino to give a talk on my abilities to foresee certain future events. I had been told that an important journalist, specialized in the paranormal, wanted to meet me. I had already heard of Paola Harris as an international investigative journalist in the Ufological field and, naturally, I was impatient to meet her. After my talk, Paola Harris came up to me and very politely asked me for an interview. I could never have refused her as I was so curious to find out more about her. Indeed, I was not mistaken as she was quite simply incredible. In that moment a strong, wonderful friendship was born which has enabled us to remain in touch despite our overburdened schedules and the distance between us.

Speaking about Paola Harris is not easy, since it would take a whole book to summarize her life and work. Rarely have I seen anyone so passionate about her various explorations, which take her to the four corners of the Earth. This passion of hers to seek the truth has led her to make exceptional discoveries and to meet "inaccessible" people, both in the United States and in Europe. Her encounters are often quite extraordinary: Edgar Mitchell (Apollo 14), John Mack, Uri Geller and Colonel Corso, to name but a few. Just by reading her first book, *Connecting the Dots*, one comes to realize the kind of work she has achieved over the past years, always with the highest standard of professionalism. Paola has traveled a great deal and I can assure you that she has spent a huge part of her life in hotels, planes and conferences, so that she is always at the right place, at the right time to gather key information for her articles.

It is the same professionalism which captivates the attention of her public at these various conferences all over the world. Paola has managed to come to prominence in her field, giving her credibility in an area which is not always favorably looked upon in today's society. Despite her success through these various diverse passages to television, books and articles which have been published in major specialist magazines, she has always kept her feet on the ground. This is quite an astonishing journey for a woman who has remained true to herself in a world which is not necessarily very easy. The world of Ufology, of the search for extraterrestrial intelligence, is probably one of the most difficult areas of research in existence today. Why?

The answer is simple! Every question mark hides a truth. If this "truth" appears to be concealed, it is because it has a role and a sense in our system of life. All the observations we can carry out regarding unexplained phenomena always give us an inkling that hidden things seem to move us further away from life's authenticity, whether through lack of information or for fear of having to rewrite the history of the world.

What is interesting about Paola Harris is that, listening to her, we very quickly realize that we do not know everything about the extraterrestrial reality. Even if some of us remain skeptical about current knowledge of the subject, it cannot be denied that certain points leave us unquestionably astounded! Advances in our knowledge in the future are bound to enable us to understand many things which at present remain unresolved. I wish the reader of this book much pleasure in entering into this subject which is, so to speak, "disturbing and unsettling."

"Reason makes no sense until the *Dream* returns to reality."

Pascal Riolo
Clairvoyant, Writer, International Speaker
Liège, Belgium, 12 November 2006 at 11.11 a.m.
http://www.pascalriolo.com

Taking Ufology Out of the Dark Ages: The Emergence of Exopolitics and the Need for Our Species to Develop a Philosophy for Eventual Contact.

For some time now, I have come to realize that we, researchers, may have remained static while the scenario around us is changing. We are still categorizing UFO sightings, which are now too numerous to mention, analyzing physical traces cases that have similar properties, and interviewing witnesses; dragging them before the media. One only needs to subscribe to George Filer's Files to see that, with the modern digital cameras, we are recording more than enough evidence of anomalous objects in the skies around the world to reach a verdict in any court of law. We are still doing the job. We are still doing the same thing, although everything around us is changing.

All this now presents us with an ethical challenge not to attribute to extraterrestrials what is terrestrial. This also presents us with a threat because, if we should ever be attacked, we would not be able to distinguish whose is the machinery, since it is virtually indistinguishable today. We need to be on our guard, not only for disinformation but also for "misidentification!" The entire scenario is becoming more apparent.

Another element that has shifted is the entire abduction scenario. Dr. Mack, in his last lecture here in Florence, Italy, in 2003, before his death, said that there seems to be a lot fewer abductions by small Grey beings. There is evidence that the alien agenda has changed and images, messages and information are being directly downloaded to people. It appears that "whatever is out there" is going directly to the people. People are coming forth with prophecies, predictions and sometimes with new scientific information and mathematical formulas. Earthly science seems to be developing in quantum leaps to join with metaphysical principles and, generally, we seem to be amalgamating the information of centuries to try to understand who we are and from whence we came. This also signifies a major shift, which he called "a new world view."

The progression of this entire study, or what we researchers claim is a study, of Ufology, is undergoing a transformation which includes the emergence of many new, young theorists, many professionally-oriented researchers and some political activists. Some of these more vocal protagonists include: Grant Cameron (Researcher on the Presidential Involvement), Richard Dolan (author of UFOs and the National Security State), Dr. Michael Salla (Author of Exopolitics), Steven Bassett (X-Conference organizer, political activist and lobbyist) and Ryan and Bob Wood (Majestic Documents (majesticdocuments.com) and Crash Retrieval Conference). This impetus has extended to college and university courses, which legitimize this research and are creating of it a new social science.

Although I have been for the most part a "Field Researcher," it is this academic element that now interests me most. There is a need to build a philosophy around contact, visitation and galactic interference in our affairs. Living in Italy for some thirteen years now and being infected by the Renaissance philosophical shift and Renaissance thinking, I have only recently begun looking at this research in an exopolitical framework, thanks to the work of Dr. Michael Salla in his new book, *Exopolitics*. Leave it to a college professor to shed some new light on what we "nuts and bolts" Ufologists have been doing for years, in my case as far back as the J. Allen Hynek years of the 1970s and 1980s. His book, *Exopolitics*, has us look at the true implications on our culture and society of this increased focus on UFOs for the last 50 years, since the "gift of Roswell!" Roswell was the turning point, as it became a race to hide the truth and create such a disinformational network that it has most of us chasing our tails. The Government is not at fault and yet we blame the mythical government, which has changed hands so many times since 1947 and which even misinforms its own presidents. We blame the military but not all the military is guilty of this massive cover-up. Some elements of the military have been trying to keep the technological and back-engineering operations under wraps but they probably do not understand the whole story themselves, nor its real implications. The right hand often does not know what the left hand is doing and the "information handlers" have all been replaced over the years.

I recently began looking at this paradigm shift in another light, since it seems that contact has changed and the agenda seems to be shifting directly to the people. There is much evidence with the witness testimony that is now emerging and with the presentation of Steven Greer's Disclosure Project and the X-Conference, both in Washington DC, that some interesting doors seem to be opening. It is now 2005 and roughly fifty years after the Holliman Eisenhower Accord. The question is: will there be a shift in consciousness, in philosophy, and will people be tired of this planetary control though fear, terrorism or otherwise? Will the military be tired of keeping secrets that, in the end, is not in its best interest in the protection of freedom? All these questions are pertinent today to what is an Earth-bound civilization of human beings who are watching one tragic Earth change after another happen, some of them consequences of their own raping of the environment.

Turning the Corner!

Lately, I have noticed a real hunger and eagerness to know the truth and a real cooperation to share information and facilitate disclosure, which is replacing the territoriality of the researchers of the past. Maybe the time has come to get on with it!

The Charles Hall case, which I cover in this book, is a major quantum leap in disclosure and expert witness testimony. It opened many doors to cooperation among different types of researchers. It began with my research of the case in July 2003, together with airline pilot, David Coote, and a LAPD-retired policeman. This research has been enhanced by the contributions of researchers all over the world who, like me, are trying to figuratively digest the fact that alien civilizations have been hosted on Earth, as early as 1965, in a cooperative technology exchange. If one is to believe ex-Air Force weather observer, Charles Hall, and the story is so rich in details that there is little reason to disbelieve him, we have had entire families of these so-called star visitors on the planet for some part of our history. Of course, Clifford Stone told me this years ago – but who is he but someone who actually was involved in crash retrievals!

The fact that people like Charles Hall, Clifford Stone, Colonel Philip Corso, Clark McClelland and other credible military witnesses are being allowed to talk makes me think that the agenda has changed and disclosure is close.

Exobiology and Exopolitics.

Will our reaction, as a species, be "shoot first and ask questions later," as the Von Braun prediction begins to unveil itself? I would be quite hesitant to begin a war with a super-galactic force and so Paul Hellyer agrees. All we know now is that we are being "watched!"

If the new "alien agenda" is to go directly to the people, then how will the people act or, better, react? (One is a carefully planned policy the other is an unprepared and often violent reaction based on fear). That is why it is so important that we weigh the exopolitical implications of this inevitable contact through examining the actual facts and testimony and past political policy.

I remember when Carl Sagan helped create the fascinating scientific field of Exobiology and he talked to us, on the NOVA programs, about the possibilities of extraterrestrial life. It was clear he knew more but logically he needed to present it in stages. It began a process of acceptance of possibilities; slow steps towards revealing the truth. As hypothetical as it was then, in the 1970s, it has become more real in this millennium with the exploration of our many interplanetary probes. Therefore, it is logical that the creation of Exobiology goes hand in hand with the creation of Exopolitics, as we, on this planet, will need to study the implications but, even more, the protocols of contact! Thanks to the pioneer work of Dr. Michael Salla and, in Canada, Alfred Webre, we can begin to plan and decide "as a species" what we are to do. We should create a philosophy but, even more importantly, a protocol and political strategy that will not be based on fear but on mutual respect. True, that not all "ET contact" may be positive but we should demand some clear indicators. Ex- Canadian Minister of Defence, Paul Hellyer mentioned this when I interviewed him in Toronto in February 2005.

This will become more important than measuring the radiation level of the soil sample or recording the radar positioning of the object in our skies. Ironically, the UFO examined could be our back-engineered technology. It is time to determine our individual positions and our own individual philosophy of contact and then look at our role as a species. It is time to develop a few academic classes in our sociology departments in our universities that will address contact and *Exopolitics*.

In the end, we need to work out a philosophy of study that can be incorporated in our academia to educate our future generations so they do not re-invent the wheel but maybe re-interpret it. Also, to eliminate this regime of "fear," we may need to return to a more naive time where we acted out of respect; to bring back the enthusiasm of the 1950s days of space exploration and, Sagan-like, wide-eyed wonderment of the Universe. With a philosophy in place, the protocol must come next. Ex-airman Charles Hall, when confronted with the physical presence of the Tall Whites, needed to decide whether to stand or run, whether to speak or shoot, whether he was sane or insane and whether he was acting as an individual or part of some established program. This is all protocol and any future contact will present us with these future dilemmas.

Someone needs to discuss this now. Someone needs to brief the planet on the agreements made. Someone needs to come clean with our real history and someone needs to help us with a new social science called Exopolitics. Carl Sagan is gone but he has left us with his legacy in the film *Contact*. Maybe we need to believe Jody Foster when she lost time-travel minutes and maybe we need to believe Charles Hall in his Indian Springs experience of co-existence with extraterrestrials; cultures like us who have children.

So the questions are: Who is in charge today? What are we to expect from our own UFO copycat technology? Where are the Aliens? Where are the crashes? Why are more credible witnesses being allowed to talk and who is now running the show? I will try to address these questions in this book but, most of all, I will try to emphasize a need for a new academic discipline to address the challenges we face in the likelihood of imminent contact. I will try to review protocols that have been used in past contact and analyze whether we, as a species, need to devise new ones. This was my goal in writing this, my second book, to present new information in the form of interviews with credible people to help stimulate critical thinking. Yes! After all this time, we are still connecting the dots.

Section One

Unconventional Wisdom
from Unconventional People

Few men are willing to brave the disapproval of their fellows, the censure of their colleagues, the wrath of their society. Moral courage is a rarer commodity than bravery in battle or great intelligence. Yet it is the one essential, vital quality for those who seek to change a world that yields most painfully to change.

Robert Kennedy (20 November 1925 – 6 June 1968)

Section One

On 23 September, 2005, in Canada, a most extraordinary event occurred in history. One courageous man, speaking at a conference at the University of Toronto said: "UFOs are as real as airplanes." He was no ordinary gentleman but the former Minister of Defence of Canada and I was supposed to be in Canada for that conference. As fate had it, I could not attend because of illness so I flew to Canada five months later to meet him and get perhaps the most important testimony of my journalistic career. He is an extraordinary man who speaks in ordinary terms and his words contain "unconventional wisdom." This section is dedicated to people of that caliber.

Interview with Former Canadian Defence Minister, Paul Hellyer

24 February 2006
Toronto, Canada

Paola: I wanted to interview the Honorable Paul Hellyer, who has come out with a speech using terms that are so unpopular in Politics. So I think we will start by asking him: When did you get interested in the whole, entire, UFO field? When were you curious about what was in the skies? Was it when you were working as Defence Minister under Lester Pierson? Was that a curiosity? Was it when you were young? When was it?

Hellyer: Not really. It is very recent. When I was Minister of National Defence, I had reports crossing my desk about sightings. They just indicated as to whether there was some natural explanation or whether there wasn't and I was far too busy at the time to worry about it very much because I was the Minister who united the Armed Forces: The Royal Canadian Army, The Royal Canadian

2

Navy and The Royal Canadian Air Force, into a single armed force. This was really unprecedented in the Western World. Robert McNamara, who was the US Secretary of Defense at the time, said this is what all the ministers wanted to do but didn't have the guts to do. It was war really to accomplish this.

Paola: This was McNamara under Kennedy in the 1960s?

Hellyer: That was the 1960s, so I was just too busy to be curious about UFOs and other things. It is only, I suppose, in very recent times, when some friends started sending me things. Frankly, I was too busy to read them, or I thought I was, so I kept putting them off and I put them on the shelf for future reference. I must admit that it was only after I took Colonel Corso's book to my little lodge in Muskoka a year ago and sat down and read it that it really tweaked my interest because I knew right away it was real. I said, "Hey! This is something I want to find out about because this is important and there are a lot of policy issues that I'm going to have to think about."

Paola: This book, who gave it to you?

Hellyer: I guess it was Pierre Juneau. Pierre has been sending me quite a bit of stuff. He is very judicious. He knows that I am overloaded and you looked at my desk earlier so you know that it is true.

Paola: But you are an activist in many, many areas.

Hellyer: That is true. Yes, I'm just going night and day. People ask me what I do now that I'm retired and the only difference is that I only work six days a week now – and it is more or less true. But I read the Corso book and I knew that it was authentic. I asked myself, you know, would anyone be capable of making that fiction? I only read a few books a year and the Corso book was so convincing that I could not make up my mind one hundred per cent until right at the end, whether it was fact or fiction. I said, "Is there any possibility that this book could be fiction?" And the answer that I concluded is, no, that it couldn't be because there were too many times, too many names, too many places and there are too many references that I would know about as the former Minister of National Defence, that I would recognize as being legitimate. All of a sudden I became deeply interested and deeply concerned.

Paola: And I also know, because it was part of a story that was written about you, that you called a four-star general in the United States to confirm....

Hellyer: I am not at liberty to say who it was or how many stars he had. When I was reading the book, my nephew asked what I was reading and I told him and so he was, like a large proportion of the population, a skeptic and did not mind admitting it. So he went away, as he had been visiting for a few days. Then a couple of weeks later he called me. He said: "I had been talking to my friend, the retired General, and I told him about the book. He said, quote: 'Every word is true and more!' "And he said, "Now I want to get my hands on that book!"

Paola: Well, the book was a best seller and it did come out programmed at the 50th anniversary of the Roswell crash. We have groups who believe that Roswell didn't even happen – where Colonel Corso, in the book and in the Dawn of a New Age, talks, which are his original notes, tells about seeing a body in Fort Riley, Kansas, in 1947. So it is not just his work at the Pentagon but it is the fact that he did also see an alien body, which is very important. So, you are telling me that this changed the way you thought about a lot of things and you were curious and you also considered it serious. Did you consider it serious because it is a matter of National Security or did you consider it serious because, as a human being, it changed the way you looked at the world?

Hellyer: It made me very curious and concerned because I understand policy issues when they stare me in the face. So I said, "There are all kinds of policy issues here." First off, General Twining, General Nathan Twining, designated these people as "enemy aliens." So my first question is: Are they still designated enemy aliens? Because if they are, then the United States Armed Forces are preparing to kill them. Then I asked myself, "If they start taking on a superior technology, what is going to happen? Are they just going to take it or are they going to retaliate? What are the consequences of such a thing for the United States and for the world?" It is just absolutely, tremendously important. And, of course, other policy considerations are, well, that if this technology is so absolutely wonderful, it has the makings of saving our planet from environmental destruction. We could get away from burning fossil fuels and save the ozone layer and stop the ice caps from melting and raising the water levels world-wide and stop disrupting the weather patterns that are upsetting a lot of people. I think upsetting them a lot more than they are willing to admit – and so this is reason two, which is tremendously important. The third one, of course, is that it certainly reinforces that the officials are not telling the truth about Roswell. I know that. I heard some of them on television not too long ago and the party line was still that it was a weather balloon and I heard dozens of others say they were sworn to secrecy. So I said, "Wait a minute! Give me a break! You are swearing people to secrecy because of weather balloon crashes?"

Paola: It is not logical.

Hellyer: Well, it is not credible! So when we are talking about these things, they can accuse the people who say that the crash was real of not being credible but I would say that the people who would say it was a weather balloon are by no means credible. So I say to myself that this cover-up, because I am convinced that there has been a systematic cover-up, a thorough and very successful cover-up for half a century or more, the whole cover-up lends credence to Lewis Latham's (the editor of Harper's Magazine) theory of the two governments. I suspect you are familiar with that?

Paola: The shadow government and the real government?

Hellyer: The permanent and the provisional. He says that the permanent United States Government is the Fortune Five Hundred list and the top legal firms of Washington that do their legal work and the top PR companies that do their public relations, or their propaganda – if you want to be a little more vulgar about it – and the top civil servants, both military and civil. They run the United States and every few years, and let me paraphrase a little bit with the license I have as a former politician, they have a charade called an election and the permanent government picks the actors to go on stage and read the scripts written by the programmed government and they try to pick actors that won't improvise too much, and who will do as they are told in effect, and then they give them the money to get elected and nobody else need apply because it has become such an expensive business, especially in the United States, where they raise these huge, astronomical amounts of money to get elected. Anyone who doesn't have the backing of the Establishment just isn't in the race. They call it Democracy but this is just nonsense. It confirms for me that we have a real problem in countries that we call Democracies, where we are basically the pawns of the people who consider themselves to be the proprietors of the orders of our society, and it does not often matter who we elect, they are not going to change anything of significance. These are fundamental policy questions that intrigue me, not just intrigue me but which I think have to be resolved first, not only for the benefit of the United States but for all mankind, because we tag along with the United States because whatever they do we are involved in. Just, I guess it is just in today's paper, our new Minister of National Defence, under the new minority government under Steven Harper, has said that they are going to reopen the question of the anti-missile defense. Right away my antennae go up. We are going become part of this business of building a system designed to take the "alien intruders" on for size. Do we want to be part of that? Do we want to be part of it without knowing what we are doing, which is obviously the case. Does our Prime Minister? Is he in the loop? Absolutely not! I'm sure he is not! Is our Minister of Defence, who is a Brigadier General, in the loop? Well I'm sure he is not. He's just going along with the conventional wisdom that we have to build a system that protects us from rogue missiles from heaven knows where; the party line, the cover stories and I say, "You know this is not good enough!" We have got to have some facts and figures and some real hard information before we start spending money and time and diverting resources from far more important things to be part of a project that probably is not good for us.

Paola: So you are for disclosure. Do you realize, you're saying that you are for *full disclosure*? It will be pulling the rug out from under a lot of institutions that are well established, including the financial, the religious and the political institutions, and that is the excuse a lot of people have been using for keeping the secret still a secret? How would you deal with that?

Hellyer: I believe in seeking the truth. In the 'Good Book' it says: "The Truth will set you free." I don't think there is any other approach.

I don't think you can live a lie. I am a religious person and I am not the least bit concerned about disclosure. And I'm absolutely determined that we find out what the truth is and I think that it is just natural and inevitable that there are other species elsewhere in the galaxy, or galaxies, that are more advanced technologically that we are, and probably more advanced spiritually as well, and we should cooperate with them and learn from them and work together to make a better world. We should start with making our world better and then we could cooperate to make a better galaxy or galaxies. These are the kinds of projects and policies we should be adopting and not trying to spend hundreds and millions of dollars when we have millions of people on our own planet dying of starvation and ill health. I put on the Scale of Justice a project costing a few hundred million dollars that happens to fit the temperament of the military industrial complex against the saving of a few hundred million lives, who otherwise are people who otherwise don't have a chance. We are just not helping, when we have the capacity and resources to help them and to give them a more abundant life.

Paola: Well, this is also entering into a philosophy. As a ufologist, I feel that we have plenty of sightings. We have been recording them forever. We have thousands and thousands. This is a phenomenon that, from South America to Europe to Asia, we have enough proof that there are sightings of these anomalous objects. Now we are into the philosophy of: "What do we do with the truth? What are the policy issues?" This goes into a brand new area that Dr. Michael Salla and Alfred Webre are interested in, called "Exopolitics." Would you agree that, even in the future, we need to get together, even in a grass roots level – since the politicians are not doing it, to develop some policies concerning contact?

Hellyer: Well, I'm sure we have to do something. I applaud them for

8

their efforts. We have to do something positive by way of cooperation and Alfred Webre suggested a ten-year period of contact and cooperation. I think that would be marvelous – and heaven only knows where it will lead. I think it would be far, far more positive than spending the next ten years trying to build the military system capable of starting an intergalactic war.

Paola: Which we might not win.

Hellyer: Well of course not, but that is a possibility that some military people would never take into account. They say we will just keep working until we win. I understand the military mind.

Paola: It is also that war makes "money." We are dealing with a complex that lives on this money-making situation.

Hellyer: It only makes money for certain people but it puts the rest of us in debt under our very peculiar monetary system which, you may or may not know, is one of my particular lifetime interests.

Paola: Yes! I see you have written other books on economics. I did not know you are so prolific in this area; books like *Surviving the Global Financial Crisis* and *Agenda, a Plan for Action.* You have written several books about the monetary system.

Hellyer: This is such a peculiar system that we expend the money to win a war. But the way we do it is by going further into debt and, consequently, every time we have another war, the people have the additional debt burden put on them, while a few people who own the munitions factories are the beneficiaries, but the beneficiaries of the munitions factories are not the ones that do the fighting. They are the ones who have luxury continuing during the wartime period. It is the ordinary people that do the fighting and lose their sons and fathers and uncles and brothers, then have to carry debt afterwards, instead of having the freedom to regroup their lives and make them better. There are some humongous policy issues involved. They are so big that I find it difficult to find words to describe them.

Paola: Now on a grass-roots level, if you were to give us advice, what would it be? We are using a lot of what you say in our Area 51 magazine because you have been courageous enough to ask President Bush to reconsider a base on the Moon and so forth. But on a grass-roots level, those people who realize that what you are saying is wise and what you are saying is really the truth, on a grass-roots level, what advice would you give us all, to do some changing, to look to a better future? You are speaking on the political level because you are speaking as someone who has a particular position but what would you advise on a grass-roots level? We, the people. What would you suggest we do?

Hellyer: I think the people should inform themselves of the information available. There is a lot of information. You were saying that the Disclosure Project drew little press.

Paola: Steven Greer's Disclosure Project had the qualifications of a very well-orchestrated "media" event, dealing with the truth about UFOs.

Hellyer: We need to use the Internet globally to spread the word and use that vehicle for the grass-roots people to demand of their politicians, some action. In Canada recently, a group of friends are asking the Senate Defence Committee to hold an inquiry and to interview some of the people present that Greer had, and some others you know, and to talk to them. I think in Canada they will get some press.

Paola: Do you think that Canada will receive outside pressure not to do that?

Hellyer: They may, but if they buckle under it will be just one more dis-
appointing aspect of our being concerned with what the white
elephant tells us to do. But if we did it here, it could provide
some pressure. The communications goes from South to North.
It is not unusual that they go North to South. Some listen to the
Canadian Broadcasting Corporation, and so forth, and if they
got enough good publicity here some of it could leak south of
the border and they could encourage to do something. I think
that they should demand of members of Congress: "What are
you doing with our money? What projects? What secret projects
are there and what are the consequences militarily?" and, "Do
you consider these people enemy aliens and, if so, why? Prove it
to us and show us the evidence." Encourage more Americans to
demand that members of Congress do something. I think the
only thing we can do is to keep putting pressure on politicians
and say, "Hey! You are elected to look after our interests not to
do what intelligence organizations tell you to do!" They are not
elected by anybody. They are not accountable to anybody. They
are just a bunch of people who think they, sort of, own the world
and have their own little club and they lie to each other – and
once you get in the habit, it spills over in what you are likely to
tell the public. We have a very great responsibility to try to put
pressure on the politicians to say the time has come: full disclosure. We want to know, and then we can decide whether we
want to embark on a project to save the planet in cooperation
with others or let you continue on the road to make bigger and
better hydrogen bombs to blow up bunkers; to do a lot of things
which will ultimately result in a virtually uninhabitable planet,
or relatively uninhabitable, and that seems to be the choice.

Paola: OK. To wrap up this interview, you had mentioned that you
are writing another book and that you are going to dedicate a

chapter to this subject. We need more of that. Can you just give us an inkling of what that chapter will say or will reflect?

Hellyer: Just basically the things that I've been saying to you. Starting with evidence of people who have a lot of experience in this area. I'm not going to give a lot of examples because you can't put much in one chapter and I do not want the book to be too long, I'd like some people to read it! To maybe get eight or ten of the most credible people who have personal knowledge and to talk to them myself, so I can quote them verbatim, and to say these are credible witnesses and I believe them to be telling the truth. I do not believe that a lot of other people are telling the truth and the time has come for full disclosure. In my own words, give the reasons why the time has come for *full disclosure.* I will develop some political aspects of this in other parts of the book, where I'll be taking about policy, including momentary policy. So there will a few threads tying this together.

Paola: Well, it is all connected. It has a "futuristic" aspect to it; a philosophy of Exopolitics, of how to deal with this reality. In other words, let's have a say in the way this goes in the future! I think that's why we are so elated that you came forward, because it gives people hope. We have to give people hope that we can design a future. Also, I wanted to ask you, when will this book come out, so we can look forward to it?

Hellyer: I think it will take the best of two years to write. I want to research it properly and I want to make it as authentic as I'm capable of making it. I have no deadline, but at the same time I want to get started as soon as possible, and get on with it. I kind of hope this is out before the next presidential election. It is not important, in a sense, but, in a sense, I may have some advice for the electorate for the kinds of alternatives that they should look at for party policy, in both the United States and Canada, and it will be my final effort I think, so I want to make it a good one and I'll try to tie together the lose ends as part of a whole.

Paola: You mentioned the United States and Canada but I wanted to add that we, in Europe, are following you very closely because whatever happens here is reflected on the other side of the ocean and I think what you have done for us is make us one global community, as far as understanding that this matter affects everybody.

Hellyer: It is a global community and everyone is affected and the monetary system is universal; I don't restrict it to North America. But these things we are talking about are universal. The fact that we have starving people in one part of the world and rich people in the other, who are overeating, is universal. This is not restricted to any geographical area, although I will concentrate on the one I know best. We can have a world of peace if we have men and women of good will. What are missing, at the moment, are men and women of good will. We are more interested in killing each other then helping each other, so if somehow we can turn that around and reset our priorities; to change the direction off our lives and expenditures to emancipate mankind and "other kind," Start with the thought: "Let's start to look forward to a positive future." Not a utopia, but something positive. And it is possible; we have the means! We have the technology; everything we need, except the political will to do it. That is what is lacking. General Eisenhower warned us about this, I guess he knew about the UFO question at the time when he said it: "Beware of the military-industrial complex," and he probably concluded that some of the information from the ETs was getting intro the wrong hands and that, somehow, we had to re-establish public control over what was going on.

Paola: Well, you have given us some hope and, in Europe, most of us are one hundred per cent behind you and we will be waiting for this book. We need to develop a philosophy of Exopolitics on a grass-roots level. Having someone of your caliber speak helps validate this exopolitical view. It will help not only us but the whole, entire planet. Thank you.

Hellyer: Let's hope we can work together and do something.

Through exopolitical activists like Alfred Webre and Dr. Michael Salla, we applaud a new decade of contact, through citizen diplomacy, with the Extraterrestrial intelligent beings who are active on and around the Earth for several decades at least and who seem to harbor no hostile or predatory designs. On the contrary, some of them at least exhibit real concern for our survival as a species and for the ecological health of the planet. Lt. Colonel Wendelle Stevens (USAF, Rtd.) is one expert who has analyzed data collected over sixty years, leading him to the conclusion that the Extraterrestrials who visit us have peaceful intentions.

The dialogue between civilizations will have to include, sooner or later, those beings and cultures that are not human, in the "homo sapiens" category, but which clearly have a presence on our planet and a stake in the future of terrestrial and human life. This issue must be brought into the mainstream. It can no longer remain confined to fringe groups of "spiritualists," "New Agers" or dedicated "Ufologists." Neither can it be left to the care of secretive and shadowy military organizations that are primarily devoted to expanding the power of the states they serve and, thereby, their own influence and resources. In his farewell message to the nation, President Eisenhower warned of the danger posed by the uncontrolled ambition and greed of the US (and transnational) "military industrial complex," Being a journalist, I find the Media more responsible for the cover-up than the Military. I find that many journalists are lacking in a sacred responsibility to print the truth, especially as it was courageously presented by the military witnesses of Steven Greer's Disclosure Project on 9 May, 2002. A moment that could have changed history was lost.

I really understood Paul Hellyer's concern that dedicated people like Dr. Steven Greer needed to be taken seriously and that the witnesses of the Disclosure Project needed to be heard, perhaps in Canada. Since I helped Steven with filming the witnesses in Italy, I realized what a huge sacrifice these people made. So I was elated when Dr. Greer went to Canada to appear with Paul Hellyer in a follow-up meeting in May 2006, five years after the Washington media event. I was hoping it would be a major media event but instead there was little media world-coverage. There are reasons for this, as Steven Greer discusses this very subject with me in his cabin in Crestone, Colorado, during Cseti training. He is, perhaps, the most powerfully-articulate man any journalist will meet. In the following interview he discusses why the censorship of the most taboo subject on Earth, UFOs.

The Death of the Fourth Estate.

2/28/11

Interview with Steven Greer, 4 July, 2005. 09-18, Crestone, Colorado. www.DisclosureProject.org www.CSETI.org.

Paola: You said you were working on three things. What are they?

Steven Greer: CSETI, the Ambassadors to the Universe program; the other is the Disclosure Project. We are still doing the Disclosure Project because we have a website with ten million people on it. People don't realize that the Disclosure Project video has been seen by more people than see CNN every night. I am still meeting with members of Congress within the last year, trying to say: "Look, this information exists and it is not only related to UFOs and extraterrestrials but also to alternative energies and propulsion systems that would solve most of our problems. So, disclosure still has to go on and we have a Disclosure Representatives Program. We have dozens of people all over the world who host Disclosure Project screenings and meetings. So that is still going on. We would love to do Disclosure II. I have yet to understand that, after we did the Disclosure Project event in 2001, we doubled the number of military assets in terms of the number of witnesses because they came out of the closet. As a matter of fact, a retired Air Force general, who has knowledge of these covert programs, is one of them. The problem is that we do not have the funding to do it. We have got to find a source of institutional support and funding to be able to do the next level of it or it's impossible to carry forward. There is no funding for anything serious and this is the tragedy of the whole UFO movement. It has become a carnival and caricature of itself yet we are dealing with incredibly important things and my understanding is that the intelligence community, which really does run the UFO subculture, wants to keep it that way. Now, what I'd like to do in the next year or two is do another level of disclosure, where we would bring in some of the new top-secret witnesses we have and government officials, including a former Clinton Administration official. Also in technology, where we can bring in scientists who can testify to the existence of sources of energy and propulsion systems and how they have been systematically acquired and suppressed by large transnational corporate interests. Most people post 9-11 really do not care if there are UFOs and ETs out there. The majority of Americans believe UFOs are real anyway. They just don't know what to make of it. You've got to connect it to something meaningful. The fact is that it is meaningful because there are enormous implications to the secrecy and the secrecy is not because of the extraterrestrial component. The secrecy is because of the technology that would make obsolete all the oil and gas and coal power in the world.

Paola: What I am saying is that it is possible that it cannot be done here. Maybe Canada. Did you even dream of doing Disclosure II in Canada?

Greer: Now, I am going to say something here that people hate to hear. You cannot do this without the dominant power, the only super-power in the world. We have projects in Norway and Canada. The dominant power is the American Transnational Corporate Machine. What I tell people is – geography is irrelevant!

Paola: But the Media would open it up there!

Greer: I think that what most people don't realize is that the issue we are dealing with has no geographical boundaries and hasn't had for decades.

Paola: We need the Media Support, don't we?

Greer: Of course. It would have the seed funding we asked for. We could have had the initial level of the Disclosure Project in Washington, then move the whole thing to Canada, and to Rome and Switzerland and these places. There was the Chinese news media that took it seriously. You cannot ignore 110 top military, top-secret guys who are cosmonauts, brigadier generals and so on. You cannot ignore these people! And the other problem is that the major media is corrupt and is the most corrupt institution in the world.

Paola: How does this affect disclosure?

Greer: If you were to ask me what is the largest problem with getting disclosure out and getting these technologies out to the world, it is not the White House, it is not the Congress, it is not the UN, it isn't the Parliament; it is the Media which, in democracies, was supposed to be the Fourth Estate, which means, one of the "watch dogs" of checks and balances to the other three branches of government: the judiciary, the executive and the legislative. That is where the Fourth Estate concept came from. I have a man who was on the board of AOL, Time Warner and CBS, who told me, in 1992, basically, "The Fourth Estate is dead! We have no Fourth Estate." I had a Washington Post reporter frankly tell me that nothing important will ever be published in the major media. Look at our website, where I talk about the Peter Jennings special, and you will see a link to a CIA document that was sent to me recently this year, that was dated 1991, during the first Bush presidency. It clearly describes, on page six, if I remember correctly, that there are assets that the intelligence community has at every major news media in the world, to kill, change or alter stories they want to control. The problem is the corruption of the news media and the lack of a truly free press at large. Now, the minor media is irrelevant. The major media is corporate and they are shills for the shadowy, transnational, para-governmental entity and the problem with that is that we are living in a pseudo-democracy, where the people cannot get the information. I have said recently that Gorge Soras and others need to come forward and put a billion or two into a "new" media empire. I said this should be called the Disclosure Network News. DNN instead of CNN and basically say, "OK. We need to be able to have the assets to pour this information into the Public to educate them to what is really going on: Corporate America, or Corporate Italy or Corporate Japan."

Why is this secrecy going on? Who is sitting on the technologies and what the truth is? It is not going to happen. The major media right now are horizontally and vertically integrated with corporate interests that do not want this information out. One of the fundamental problems with the notion that we are living in a democracy without a free press, without a truly free press that is not corrupted by these secretive interests, is that it is very difficult for the masses to know what is really happening. For that reason, it makes a mockery out of Democracy. It is interesting that I'm talking about this on 4 July. I think that what everyone has to understand is that we have to get some seriously committed people: financially, professionally and with talent in the media, to say, "Look! We really have to do some serious exposés. For instance: this AOL executive told me that some of the secret UFO Documents he gave to Mike Wallace, of 60 Minutes TV show, the most famous investigative reporting show in the world, who wanted to do a special. Mike Wallace was considering doing something on it but they pulled the plug on it.

During the Disclosure Project event, the executive producer of ABC News, who was the final call guy on Primetime Live and 20/20, told me he wanted to do an hour special involving these top-secret witnesses. A few weeks later I called him on that and I asked, "What are you doing on that?" and he said, "Well they won't let me do it!" "Who are they?" He replied, "Dr. Greer, you know who they are!"

I have seen this up close and personal with the world's media, not just with the US media. I have seen it with the BBC in England and other countries. The inability for even people who are highly placed within the news media to be unable to be allowed by their corporate masters to tell the truth is appalling. So, since we do not have a truly free media, the Fourth Estate has been assassinated essentially. You have a mockery of democracy because that is the "Check and Balance" system that is no longer there.

An Exopolitical Consideration and a Challenge for Researchers

I will pose the question of recognition of UFO sightings. After 60 years of serious back-engineering of alien craft, we need to ask ourselves if what we are seeing in the skies is "our stuff" or "their stuff." What criteria do we use to decide this? For the answer to this, I went to two experienced authorities: one on UFOs, and crash retrievals, and one a NASA engineer who worked 22 years on all the Apollo missions. Clark McClelland told me that he was alerted that he would see these craft when he went to Belize on vacation in 1995. They were two flying saucers that flew one in the wake of the other. He has the incredible graphics on his website: www.stargate-chronicles.com.

"Personally, I believe that the Onion Drive technology is flying in the skies of earth each day. I observed two over Belize in 1995 and two more about a month ago, over my town in Florida. Advanced weapons systems are developed about 20, 30 to 40 years prior to the release of such technology to the world public. The people on Earth have no knowledge what advanced crafts are flying in the skies and are going to the Moon, Mars and beyond." Clark C. McClelland, former ScO, Space Shuttle Fleet, Kennedy Space Center, Florida, 1958 to 1992.

To Moon, Mars and beyond! Oh, Oh, Houston! We have a real problem here in 2007 with UFO sightings, because we civilians can't tell the difference. However, we know it is useless to invent more organizations to archive them. We have been doing that for years and we know the phenomenon exists. We may be recording our stuff that indeed DOES go faster than the speed of light.

At conferences recently, I show astounding, close-up film footage of a craft coming out of a forest, doing two 360-degree turns in front of a cameraman, who has a video camera on a tripod, and then it jets off into the sunset at light speed. This place is Ponte di Giulio, in the Veneto region of Italy, near the NATO base of Aviano. That area is a military area where soldiers practice maneuvers and I do not think aliens were invited to visit and see the show.

The film footage was analyzed in Hollywood and the object on the screen is "real"; but real military or real alien is the question? Which? In this new decade of research we will have many more challenges like this. Ironically, those who see this footage argue to the death that it is alien because they love the idea of a close encounter like this.

I am convinced that some, if not most, of the craft we are seeing in 2006 are our own back-engineered, top-secret aircraft. I have an astounding interview with Ed Rothschild Fouche, who worked at Area 51, in my first book *Connecting the Dots: Making sense of the UFO Phenomena*. He spoke about the triangular antigravity TR3B that is a back-engineered, triangular alien craft that can easily be mistaken for a UFO. Was the Belgium sighting the TR3B – and why would this aircraft be flown through a populated area, risking damage to civilians and villages? Many triangular craft have been seen, while they have been flight-tested over the Area 51 Nellis Ranges, by researchers and responsible citizens. Some say the Phoenix triangle craft, part of the Phoenix Lights phenomena, could also be exotic technology. Arizona Researcher, Jim Dilettoso, who examined the video and still photographs, does not agree. He says that Dr. Lynn Kitei, who filmed it, saw the orange "orbs" detach and attach themselves to this huge-shaped craft which was the size of several football fields. So we can assume this was "their stuff," especially since flying a craft this size over the huge, populated area of Phoenix, Arizona, to have so many amateur video camera operators film it, would be absurd.

Another case in point to examine might be the Rendlesham Forest, Bentwaters case. One NASA engineer told me that was probably the TR3B advanced aircraft checking the security of the US nuclear arsenal in England. But from the witness testimony of Larry Warren and Charles Halt, it is obvious that the craft was having flying difficulties and the military men were terrified at this incident. Most of them were also intensely debriefed right after it happened. If this was our surveillance craft, why was the head commander of the Bentwaters base not warned? For the answer, I went to Clifford Stone. Sergeant Clifford Stone, who worked on crash retrievals with recovery projects Moon Dust and Blue Fly, told me in a telephone conversation on 2nd of January 2000, that he was in Germany at the time and the Bentwaters case was a real UFO case. We will see further on that Dr. J Allen Hynek was investigating previous sightings there as early as 1956. How interesting to tie this all together. There is a reason something interests these visiting civilizations at Bentwaters near Rendlesham Forest which in itself is a mystical location.

The case is fascinating and, as destiny would have it, I actually heard from a participant and witness, who was on the Bentwaters Base in England at the time. Steve LaPlume now lives in China and having heard me on the *Coast to Coast* show with George Noory, in 2005, he contacted me immediately and trusted me with the following testimony:

"I, Steven Robert LaPlume, on this third day of February 2005, wish to declare the following as true regarding the events on and at RAF Bentwaters from December 26th, 1980 to January 30th, 1981.

I witnessed members from another flight entering the day room at about 10:00 a.m., three hours after their shift ended. They were very distraught when asked about their encounter with a UFO the shift before.

Also, Larry Warren related to me the events of a few nights, which entailed the sighting of a UFO, the fact that the lights were not working properly and also that he witnessed a craft, 3 beings, and a Colonel communicating with the beings. He also mentioned that there was film documentation and that parts were flown in from Germany to help fix the downed craft. This was in early January of 1981.

I had a subsequent sighting which brought out a mass of high-ranking officials, one of which brought his wife and teenaged son to: "Hopefully get to see one this time!" [Quote by the Lt. Colonel's wife]. The base commander, Colonel Gordon Williams, (promoted by Congress the day before to General), was also present and I advised him my post was then "safe and secure," as instructed by my shift commander, Lt. Englund.

After Larry Warren came up missing for a few days and told me of his "interrogation procedure" and I confirmed I was being followed by still-unknown (to me) agents, I felt it in my best interest to trash my career, loose face with my father, a military man since World War II, and leave the base and the US Air Force for my own personal safety. I felt so strongly of this, I faked a suicide attempt and cut open my own stomach to prove my point and receive a discharge, which I did. I have no regrets over this action.

My personal thoughts are that if there was something, it was a threat to the ordinance we housed at the base. If there was nothing, then there was mass hysteria and the entire squadron of Security Police was mentally unfit to be in the position of responsibility we were charged with. If there was nothing, then why would the Assistant Base Commander of Woodbridge bring his family out to take pictures of a UFO, if there was nothing there to begin with? And why would a recently promoted General Williams get out of bed at midnight to come investigate as well?"

November 4th 1980 – April 10th 1981
By Steven Robert LaPlume – Airman First Class assigned to the 81st
Security Police Squadron

This is powerful testimony from a first-hand witness and that is the only testimony I usually consider valid, so when people always ask me if I "believe in UFOs," I say it is not a matter of belief. People see them. There is hard evidence. I cannot ignore this testimony or any testimony given to me by military or ex-military witnesses. I have been lucky that I have been able to speak to people, like Sgt. Clifford Stone at his home, informally on several occasions; that they trust me to give an accurate account of their disclosure testimony.

The Hynek Method of Study.
Laugh, Laugh, Study, Study.

I never knew how much he really knew from what he told us, his friends. He probably knew more than he could say but he would never raise his voice. He once autographed for me a paper he has written called *The UFO Phenomena: Laugh Laugh, Study, Study*. Little did he know I would write this book. J. Allen Hynek was my true inspiration. He would never attack his detractors in public. He would never make harsh judgments. He would never give you a final decision. Allen, as we called him, was a true "gentleman." He would listen to all our ideas. It always amazes me how those, who never personally knew J.Allen Hynek, attempt to write about him. He remained forever embarrassed by the "swamp gas" hypothesis.

No, he did not always represent the official party line Ufology, but I found him extremely progressive. If he wanted to represent national party line Ufology, Hynek would have remained with Project Blue Book, the United States Air Force study. He received much criticism in his life for his hesitation to cross over to the other side. But then he had six mouths to feed and a brilliant astronomy career as a professor to think about. For all our adoration of science and scientists, we know few who can really risk their funding to tell the world the truth. It is they who keep the secret and maintain the status quo.

It is useless to portray science as legitimizing Ufology and Allen would tell you that. He was an uncommon scientist, as it was he who told me that the UFO realty was filled with paranormal phenomena and that I needed to reconsider that fact in my final assessment. In the beginning, I did not agree as I was a "nuts and bolts" researcher. I now admit that it scared me and it was not until later that I realized that this element, the paranormal factor, is the one that drives scientists crazy. They cannot measure this dimension in any laboratory.

My life with Allen Hynek began when I walked into the CUFOS offices in Evanston, Illinois, in 1981, and asked if I could see how he organized the files; files that he considered anomalies from his "Blue Book" days. He quickly gave me a guided tour, asked if I wanted to be trained as an investigator and asked if I could translate all the Italian sightings. Within a month, he bought me a typewriter and sent boxes of files to my

Boulder, Colorado house. He would visit often and bring his wife Mimi and sometimes other guests. One time he brought Jenny Randles and we spoke about the Bentwaters case over dinner. Many times we would talk into the night about the obstacles he had to overcome and the resentment of other investigators, who thought he came on board too late. He really loved to network with people and, having the same star sign, so do I. He traveled all around the world and was very loved and respected. I was trained first in Chicago, as a Field Investigator, and I had a CUFOS identification card. I was privileged enough to be very close to his private secretary, Estelle Postolle. She was amazing, as she knew him well and helped enormously in the office. We worked closely when I would fly into Chicago, or rather Evanston, to be trained as an investigator but, like all of us then, we were looking for the real privileged information.

Allen Hynek was a renegade and a free thinker and we were both Taurus with Sagittarius risings. He came in with Halley's Comet and exited with it in 1986. I knew him and his wife Mimi very well, as they were my dear friends when I lived in Boulder, Colorado, in the 1980s. One year we went on vacation together in Santa Fe, New Mexico, and I took some fine portraits of them but I think I had a sense of history about this meeting as Allen died some time later and that vacation was a "gift" in our communal experience. I remember dancing the Tango with him, while my companion, Russ, danced with Mimi. Allen was a fine dancer and a fine gentleman.

The in-fighting among UFO researchers continues and it seems impossible, in this world of jealousies and envy and personal aggrandizement, to work together. So much so, that Colonel Philip Corso once said, in his statement, that the Government did not need debunkers and disinformation techniques since the Ufologists fight among themselves and do it well. He told me that the lack of cooperation and hash judgments will delay the disclosure for who-knows-how-long, to the government's amusement.

Allen Hynek would be sad today to see this because a *united front* brings strength. In the letter below, we see Dr Hynek interested in the Bentwaters sightings of 1956 and we see his very personal exchanges with James McDonald, a man, described by his wife in the interview below, as an early pioneer in this field. So whether 1956 sightings or the previously mentioned or the1980 Bentwaters UFO landing, Allen Hynek investigated them carefully as we see from these declassified letters from Blue Book archives.

Dr. Hynek's Inquiry into the Bentwaters and Lakenheath Sightings.

Letter from Capt. Gregory to J. Allen Hynek, 26 Nov, 1956
Box 9703
1125th FAG (ATIC)
Wright-Patterson AFB
Ohio

26 November, 1956
Dr. J. Allen Hynek
Smithsonian Astrophysical Observatory
60 Street
Cambridge 38, Massachusetts

Dear Dr. Hynek:

Reference is made to my letter of 20 November, 1956, in which I stated that I would send you the finalized material on the UFO case. Enclosed you will find AF 112 on the final investigations regarding this sighting. I am relieved to find that they carry it under an 'unclassified' category. This, of course, helps us in both the discussion and transmittal aspects.

I have included a rough plot of the three radar and one visual observations of the sightings. This should be of some help for your review and comment. These sightings, in my opinion, cannot be considered concurrent with respect to time. The separate report of each observer indicates three widely divergent tracks. An attempted intercept by American airplanes, which lasted for 45 minutes, produced no physical evidence of any UFO in the area. The visual observation leads me to believe that the observer was seeing Mars. Also, there appears to have been some contact (I do not wish to use the word 'collusion') between the operators of two radar stations, since they both state speed of exactly 4000 m.p.h.

I feel, therefore, that our original analyses of anomalous propagation and astronomical is more or less correct. I will consider this case closed upon receipt of your final comment, at which time I will make a compiled, final conclusion for the Air Force.

A word concerning your proposed visit. As things are now it seems improbable that any plans can be made before the beginning of January.

Sincerely
s/s Capt. Gregory

Blue Book memorandum by Dr. J. Allen Hynek 17 Oct, 1956, T56-24219

Classified CONFIDENTIAL, changed to UNCLASSIFIED, effective 15 March, 1968, under the authority of AFR 205-1, para 2-176 (ii), by Maj. Hector Quintanilla Jr.

MEMORANDUM FOR RECORD
SUBJECT: (C) Evaluation of Lakenheath Reports

1. The original Lakenheath reports and the preliminary evaluations made by ATIC were submitted to the undersigned for examination, evaluation and comment. Writer requested permission to discuss these with Dr. F.L.Whipple, Harvard University, and director of the

Smithsonian Astrophysical Observatory, in view of the fact that the sightings occurred at the time of Perseid meteors and Dr. Whipple is a world-recognized authority on meteors. Following comments will accordingly be invited to cover the three points separately.

2. It is to be regretted that so unusual a sighting report did not contain more factual material on which to base an evaluation. The Lakenheath report is one of the more unusual reports, involving electronic and visual observations and subsequent pursuit by fighter plane. Yet, report does not state whether it was definitely established that visual and electronic sightings referred to same object, or even if they occurred precisely simultaneously. Further, report does not give exact weather information, which might enable one to charge weather conditions with any precision relative to "anomalous propagation," such as frequently occurs with radars.

3. It would be of extreme value to have independent statements from the various observers, both at Bentwaters and Lakenheath. Report states that observers were traffic controllers and intelligence specialists. An analyst would be greatly aided by having independent statements from such highly trained observers, as the original report indicates the observers were.

4. The implication of the original report is that the objects were sighted simultaneously by ground-visual, air-electronic and ground-electronic means. Yet, report nowhere states stellar magnitude of visual sightings or nature of radar blips. Angular rate of motion of objects is likewise not included.

5. With the above in mind, the preliminary report submitted by Capt. Gregory covers the case as well as it possibly could under the circumstances. The present writer, upon more detailed examination of the report, and accepting the implications of the original report in the absence of specific statements, is led to differ somewhat from preliminary report. It seems highly unlikely, for instance, that the Perseid meteors could have been the cause of the sightings, especially in view of the statement of observers that shooting stars were exceptionally numerous that evening, thus implying

that they were able to distinguish the two phenomena. Further, if now any credence can be given to the maneuver of the objects as sighted visually and by radar, the meteor hypothesis must be ruled out.

6. Meteors, however, as pointed out by Capt Gregory, can lead to radar returns because of the ionization of the gases in their trail. Accordingly it would be extremely important to know whether the Bentwaters and Lakenheath radars have ever, in the past, observed meteors on their scopes and, if so, how such returns differ from the blips reported.

7. Dr. Whipple and the writer discussed the Lakenheath incident at length and Dr. Whipple pointed out immediately the statement "radars reported these facts to occur at later hours than the ground observers." This statement needs clarification, inasmuch as it contradicts other portions of the report, which indicate that, at least at certain times, visual and radar sightings were simultaneous.

8. Dr. Whipple stated that, as far as the report at hand is concerned, no obvious physical solution is suggested. He deplored the inadequacy of the typical UFO report as a scientific document. He further stated that the nature of such reports is not likely to change and urged that if the Air Force is serious in its attempts to resolve this problem, both scientifically and in the public mind, that the Air Force does more than continue its passive investigational attitudes. He suggested that, as in any scientific procedure, facts are the raw material from which one must work and that, in general, the investigator in any particular case must assume an active role in the obtaining of scientific data. In short, Dr. Whipple asked the writer whether the Air Force had ever considered, or was now considering, the possibility of initiating, for a limited time, an actual sky patrol by photographic and visual means of precisely those areas from which the maximum UFO reports originate. The writer responded that this had indeed been suggested in the past but that because of considerations of expenses and of possible public misinterpretation, it was abandoned.

9. Dr. Whipple urged that a more modest proposal of the same gen-

eral type be considered at this time. For instance, an area from which numerous reports have come in might be patrolled by a dozen or so "fish-eye" cameras, operating automatically, which would give a total record of all bright moving objects at night within a given area or sector. A simple timing device would suffice to yield the angular rate of objects in motion so that fireballs (bright meteors) could be distinguished from airplanes and from other astronomical objects.

10. The present writer submits that it might be of considerable potential use to the Air Force to be able to state, at some future time, that a careful patrol of an area "rich in UFO reports" had been accomplished and nothing of a mysterious character photographed. This would be especially true if, during the time of the patrol, UFO reports from untrained observers continued to come in from that area.

s/s J. Allen Hynek
Dr. J. Allen Hynek

Smithsonian Astrophysical Observatory
USAF UFO Scientist-Consultant
17 October 1956

Letter from Dr. J. Allen Hynek to Dr. James E. McDonald, 11 September 1970

Dr. James McDonald
Department of Atmospheric Sciences
The University of Arizona
Tucson, Arizona 85721

Dear Jim,

I have been going over your Lakenheath article in FSR. I have gotten out my files on the case and, incidentally, if you are still interested in the names that were razor-bladed out of your copy, the A/2c was John L.Vaccars, Jr. [sic] and the Technical Sergeant was Elmer L. Whenry. The names of the two interceptor pilots were First Lieutenant Charles V. Metz and First Lieutenant Andrew C. Rowe. Incidentally, also, I personally dismissed the meteor hypothesis immediately, as is pointed out in the Condon Report, page 255 of the Bantam edition.

However, all that aside, maybe you have some information that I don't have about the case, namely the thing that would tie down the passage of an object from east to the west, directly over Bentwaters, simultaneously visually by the tower operators and by the pilot overhead at 4,000 feet. In the letter to Condon, all we have is a third-hand statement. The writer states, "He said the tower reported seeing it go by..." So the writer is telling us that he heard from somebody else that the tower operator told him.

Now the Bentwaters report, which covers the period 2120Z to 2220Z, says nothing about an object passing directly overhead, although Vaccars indicates that at 2130, for a period of 30 seconds, he saw something go from 25 to 30 miles east-southeast of Bentwaters and fly on a constant course of 295 degrees to 15 to 20 miles west-northwest of Bentwaters. This could indicate that it passed overhead, but nothing is said of the object disappearing from the scope which would mean that it did not pass directly overhead, for it would have disappeared for a short time if that were the case.

The Lakenheath Report states that at 2255, Bentwaters sighted an object 30 miles east of station and that this object did disappear 2 miles east of station and then appeared 3 miles west of station. But now comes the catch: "Tower personnel at Bentwaters reported to GCA that a bright light passed over the field east to west at terrific speeds and at about 4,000 feet altitude." But at no place is it indicated that this was at 2255. The next paragraph goes on: "At the same time, pilot and aircraft at 4,000 feet. . ." That "at the same time" seems to me to refer not to 2255 but to the time the Tower personnel reported the bright light passing over the field.

31

Have you in any way been able to establish that the radar and visual sightings were indeed simultaneous? This would be a most important point in this whole thing and I, indeed, hope that you can. Nothing in my records, however, really pins this down.

I wonder whether the 2255 might in itself be in error? It seems that with all the things going on at Bentwaters from 2120 to 2220, that Lakenheath would certainly have been alerted earlier than 2255. Yet, the letter to Condon indicates that Lakenheath was not alerted until they had sighted the target going directly over them. Two points: why would have Bentwaters waited so long to alert Lakenheath and secondly, why is not the 2255 observation (if it is real) appearing in the report from Captain Holt and approved by Major Bixel? In that report it is stated, "Most significant are the reports of three sources of UFO beams tracked on the Bentwaters GCA radar." It seems to me that it would have been much more significant to have reported the simultaneous visual radar sighting because a visual object swooping by at low altitude and observed from the ground and from, and below, an aircraft, and simultaneously tracked on radar would have been far more significant than the radar alone sightings between 2120 and 2220. What do you think?

If the 2255 should, indeed, be 2155, it would tie in with the first period of Bentwaters sightings (if there were two periods) but why, in this case, would not Captain Holt have mentioned it?

Any light that you can shed on this most important case would be appreciated.

I am pleased that you did mention in your article, my memorandum, which strongly urged "that further information on the technical aspects of the original observation be obtained, without loss of time. . ." Needless to say, nothing whatever was done and you would have had to know Captain Gregory. ...... (his one and only aim in life was to become Major) and he certainly was not going to do anything whatever to go against the Pentagon, which had been told in no uncertain terms by the Robertson Panel that there was nothing to the whole subject. But then, you never have understood this and probably never will. Or perhaps you are beginning to understand somewhat as you note that your serious, strong, and I might say even emotional, attempts to have the military and the scientific establishment take the subject seriously, have not exactly met with outstanding success. And yet the climate for acceptance today is, in my opinion, an order of magnitude more favorable.

One thing I will always have to thank you for and that is the day you came to my office and pounded the desk and said, "Allen, how could you sit on this data for 18 years and not let us know about it?" It was like a revelation to me. Here, at last, was finally one real scientist who was taking the subject seriously! Up to that point, I was becoming obsessed with the idea that "everybody was out of step but Johnny" and it was a great spiritual uplift to find, at long last, another scientist seriously looking at it. I will freely admit that I originally approached the subject very skeptically for the first decade or so, largely because, as you well know, Blue Book data were so abysmally poor and no attempt was ever made to upgrade them, even when I repeatedly suggested this. So, despite your criticisms, I do have much to thank you for and I hope we may work together productively in the future.

Sincerely yours
s/s J. Allen Hynek
Director
JAH/al CC: Charles Bowen

Interview with Betsy McDonald Wife of Dr. James McDonald, Early Pioneer in UFO Research.

At the X-Conference. 23 April 2005.

"He did say that if UFOs were hostile, it would maybe unite people around the world as human beings, rather than fighting one another, UFOs should be studied." Betsy McDonald

Paola: Did you know Dr. J. Allen Hynek?

Betsy McDonald: No. I never met him.

Paola: Did your husband ever talk about him?

Betsy McDonald: Oh yes. I remember when Mac first met him and the fact that Hynek was not as open as Mac thought he should be. He told him that he shouldn't be afraid.

Paola: Did he think it was fear?

Betsy McDonald: I remember it was fear. Hynek had a daughter in college and he was worried that he had to put her through College and he thought his work would have some repercussions. Mac told him not to worry and that he should not be afraid.

Paola: Was your husband upset with the Condon report?

Betsy McDonald: Oh yes, definitely.

Paola: Did he demonstrate that at home?

Betsy McDonald: Oh yes. I sort of remember there was a memo by a person [named] Lore, that proved that Condon had basically agreed to debunk UFOs.

Paola: Who was the Memo by again?

Betsy McDonald: Lore. You know, when the Government was going to be giving a grant of, I think, a half a million dollars, for the investigation of UFOs, I remember saying to Mac, "Well, you are the most prominent person doing work on UFOs. It should go to you!" Instead, it went to Condon. I told him, "This is what happens to you. Every time you do the work, then somebody else gets the money."

Paola: Well, he was doing honest work, Betsy. Was he afraid? Did he ever come home saying, "This is making me nervous"?

Betsy McDonald: No! He thought it should all be open and above board. It was a scientific question. That was his point. That was his mission in a sense, I think, as far as UFOs are concerned. He wanted to make it a scientific question that should be taken up by science. As a matter of fact, he tried to get the National Science Foundation to take it up. He didn't succeed in that.

Paola: What was the reason they gave him that they wouldn't take it up?

Betsy McDonald: I don't recall the details. Basically that was his ideal. He went around to meteorological societies, engineering societies and other scientific bodies. He was trying to show that this should be considered a scientific question.

Paola: It is a scientific question. He thought that there should be observation posts created around the world for sightings, right?

Betsy McDonald: For sightings.

Paola: What his title? He was a physicist?

Betsy McDonald: His title was that he was a senior scientist at the Institute for Atmospheric Physics. He came to the University of Arizona to found the Institute of Atmospheric Physics, but he was not the administrative type. He was a researcher.

Paola: That is very interesting. He was a courageous man. Did he know he was going to be a hero when he was working at this? That he was working against the grain?

Betsy McDonald: My husband was naive about this. He was idealistic. People had been talking about the conspiracy. I often think of his philosophy as the "philosophy of the enlightenment." In the early days in Capitalism, everyone was optimistic about the Ideal. If you tell the truth, they will accept it and work on it.

Paola: So he had the idea that if we tell the truth then they would work on it. So he was, basically, into Truth!

Betsy McDonald: Right. That's the way he was!

Paola: So he never saw this as a matter of National Security, that these vehicles were so advanced that they could pose a threat to the United States? He never saw that?

Betsy McDonald: No. He did say, when he spent a lot of time in UFO research and it was separate from his job, that if they were hostile it would maybe unite people around the world as human beings, rather than fighting one another.

Paola: Then we would have a common enemy? Did he think they were hostile?

Betsy McDonald: No! He did not say that. What he said was: "They should be studied."

Paola: Did he leave materials behind? Did he want to write any books on UFOs?

Betsy McDonald: No, he made speeches and wrote articles.

Paola: Who are some of the people he admired most in the field?

Betsy McDonald: I don't know. He worked in NICAP a lot. He liked Dick Hall. He admired Bob Wood. He was with McDonald Douglas, you know. There were not too many people in the field then.

Paola: What years are we talking here?

Betsy McDonald: He died in 1971, so it was the late 1960s – early 1970s when he did his work. He did a lot of cases. He had gone to *Project Blue Book* when Project Blue Book closed. He stayed there a day or two and picked out about a hundred cases that he thought would be the best to study, with radar, multiple witnesses and so forth. So he had some cases when he died and there wasn't really anybody to do them. The only person that I gave the copies to was in Australia but I never heard from him again. He was a scientist, because Mac was counting on science to do it.

Paola: I hesitate to touch the question of your husband's death because everybody has about a hundred questions around it. Do you have any particular feeling about that?

Betsy McDonald: Well, it was a complicated thing. He had been suicidal before... before he studied UFOs, so that was in his makeup.

Paola: He was very intelligent. A lot of people who have a certain intelligence are very sensitive.

Betsy McDonald: I would say he was accomplished. Ann Druffel wrote about him extensively in the book *Firestorm*, by Granite Publishing.

Paola: In his lifetime, were the people he worked with sincere, like him?

Betsy McDonald: Well, they are politicians! There was an interest, I think. At times, more came out than comes out now, from what I hear at this conference (The X-Conference). More was published then.

Paola: More came out but the public was misinformed. Today, the public is informed but the government is not coming out anymore. If they came out, they would just have to admit it; so let's not play any more games, because the public is informed now. So if they had something to come out with, it would just be the admission. It would be nothing else. The admission that we have the evidence.

Betsy McDonald: Probably, but my husband was an independent scientist who was not tied in with any of the business interests or corporations or outside interests, which influence people today. It was an earlier time. He still had to get grants. He got a Navy grant. He had been in the Navy. He lost that grant doing UFO work. He lost it when he went to Australia and it was made public. The Grant was dropped in the late sixties, when the Australian newspapers reported that he was discussing UFOs with Australians.

Paola: So he suffered financially because of this, too? Did he ever have a sighting himself? Ever?

Betsy McDonald: No! He would have told me.

Paola: Have you ever had a sighting?

Betsy McDonald: No!

Paola: So his interest purely comes from scientific curiosity?

Betsy McDonald: A lot of people that he respected had, and they would tell him that they had, sightings. They came to him because he was very open and people would come to him and tell him. That is when he became interested.

Paola: If you had to tell the world something about your husband, James – you called him Mac – what would you tell them that, if he were standing here, he would want you to tell them?

Betsy McDonald: He was a scientist. He was idealistic. A person of great honesty, of great integrity and great energy. He was like Don Quixote because, in a sense, he did not understand the nature of this government cover-up. He idealized it. He worked with people that were within the government. He considered it the responsibility of the scientists to look for the answers.

Paola: Thank you, Betsy. You are very kind to talk to us!

I thank Mrs. McDonald for this interview for, in light of her husband's suicide, I came to know his courage through her. Allen Hynek also respected him and this exchange shows the caliber of scientists interested in a serious study of this phenomena. But they are not all scientists, as we will see in the next interviews. They are people who are aware; awake on a cosmic level. There are so many men, women and children involved on a planetary level.

After living in Rome, Italy, for the last fourteen years, I am witness to this. This year I spoke in Rome and Torino in Italy, in Marseilles and Argelles sur Mer in France, in Locarno and Lugano in Switzerland, in Düsseldorf in Germany, in Lincolnshire and Blackpool in England and intelligent people the world over are asking the same obvious questions. It is amazing how much of the UFO literature they read and how many Internet sites carry information. My website is translated into Italian, German, French and English.

It came as a surprise that, sometime in November, we, in Exopolitics, heralded the speech of Mr. Côme Carpentier de Gourdon, given in Greece at a conference. He is a statesman, not a Ufologist, not a scientist, and he says, and I quote from The Case for Exopolitics: Ushering in a Cosmic Dialogue:

"EXOPOLITICS, insofar as it concerns the issue of mankind's contacts with intelligent non-human life forms originating outside our planet, has an already long history. Since Antiquity, human beings have pondered this existential question: "Are we alone in the universe?" and

39

have sought to answer it according to their experience, intuition or imagination, with fear, hope, humor or incredulity."

We can see in this speech that Côme Carpentier de Gourdon has done his homework when he says:

"Some of the many covert government projects dedicated to the UFO subject in North America were ANGEL DUST, TWINKLE, POUNCE, GRUDGE, MOONDUST, MAGNET (in Canada, from 1950 to 1954, which led to the creation of a "flying saucer" detection station at Shirley Bay near Ottawa, funded by the Canadian Federal Government from 1952 to1954), BLUE FLY and others, for monitoring, reporting on and capturing or retrieving alien objects, controlled by the CIA, NSA, Navy, Air Force, etc...(more than 1000 pages of official documents have been released under FOIA regarding MOONDUST and BLUE FLY)."

He names them all and talks about the over-abundance of testimony, especially of the astronauts:

"A surprisingly high number of military officers of several countries, including 3-star generals, air marshals and admirals, not to mention astronauts in the Apollo program (Russell Schweikart, Brian O'Leary, Buzz Aldrin, Scott Carpenter among others) have admitted publicly to having seen, or been shown, evidence of UFOs that, in their best judgment, could not have been of human, terrestrial origin.. .. NASA astronaut Edgar Mitchell, statement to the Press in 1999. Mitchell, a member of the Disclosure Project has acknowledged publicly that he knows of a "UFO-cover-up" engineered and kept by what he calls a "cabal of insiders" within the US Government. An indirect confirmation has been given by New Mexico Governor, Bill Richardson, who recently officially asked the Federal Government to release the true facts pertaining to the Roswell 1947 episode, so far without success."

Ironically, this interview with Dr. Edgar Mitchell was done in Roswell, New Mexico. Dr. Mitchell is a personal friend, one of those wise men with unconventional wisdom because he surpasses the confining boundaries of scientific research when he discusses "Quantum

Cosmology"! He is honest and wants the planet to progress on its evolutionary path and he does include that "paranormal phenomena" that Allen Hynek once told me not to overlook.

Interview with Dr. Edgar Mitchell Apollo 14

Roswell 5 July, 2004

"I think I've reached the point that I'm convinced enough of the reality of the ET presence and I'm not going to deny it and shy away from it....... It is time to open this up to the public.

Astronaut Edgar Mitchell, Apollo 14

Paola: It is a pleasure to see you here in Roswell. I think that you said that you grew up in this area. I think you said that you lived here when you were about 3 to 13 years old?

Mitchell: I lived here from when I was five until I went off to College. We had a family business in the valley. It was between Roswell and Artesia.

Paola: Friends talked you into coming to speak here at the UFO museum?

Mitchell: I resisted for a long time.

Paola: Did you resist because it was connected with the UFO phenomenon?

Mitchell: No. I think I've reached the point that I'm convinced enough of the reality of the ET presence and I'm not going to deny it and shy away from it. I don't get into it in detail. That is not my area.

Paola: I know that your area is more the metaphysical.

Mitchell: Well, I think it is an interaction there. Particularly since there does seem to be a non-local communication or mental tie here with some of these functions; whether they are real or not, I don't know.

Paola: Can I ask you, why is it they pick you of all the astronauts? In the media you have been selected as one who represents the astronauts' testimony as to this UFO reality, although you mentioned you never saw one in space. Gordon Cooper talks a lot more about it in his book *Leap of Faith*. So why you? Is it by talking about the metaphysical they have attached you to the weirdness factor?

Mitchell: I think it was the personal connection, since I had personal contacts in this area. I think it is my credibility as a scientist. I am very, very incredulous about what I see. I can't throw caveats in. I don't make blanket statements. Although my experience is not first hand experience, I have become a spokesman for my colleagues who did have first hand experience. I am very clear about all of these things and I am very clear about where our lack of knowledge is. What is the frontier? What are the unknowns? What are the parameters that we don't understand? I think this gives me a lot of credibility.

Paola: What advice would you give those serious researchers that want an answer and, let's say, dream of harmony with cosmic cultures? What advice would you give them?

Mitchell: We are dealing with a difficult process here. The main problem is that we, as an Earth civilization, have not come to understand ourselves; see ourselves in a cosmic sense at all. We are still very provincial. We fight over religion. In my opinion, fundamentalist Christians are just as bad as fundamentalist Islam and, at the very core, neither religion is like that. In the inner core of both of them, these religions talk about qualities like Love and Brotherhood.

Paola: You are saying that there are more similarities than differences?

Mitchell: Of course. It's the cultural differences. It is not an intrinsic difference. It is like I said in my talk last night: "the transcendent experience is common to every culture in the world" and the transcendent experience is Brotherly Love, Nature, Harmony, the Unity, and cultures, in trying to define it, try to define an external deity as opposed to the process.

Paola: It is easier that way because you don't have any responsibility. I guess a proverb could be: You can blame it on the devil or God. It is a lack of taking responsibility for who we are.

Mitchell: Well, that's right, and our ignorance, and it is based on the egos we have. It is the unwillingness to go beyond ego. Transcendence gets you beyond ego. If you go beyond ego, you see all of this in a more decent perspective and you can start to put all pieces together. We haven't done that yet. Not as a civilization.

Paola: That is why you think that contact is not likely until we get there. Right? Humanity as a species is not there. You mentioned in your talk yesterday, if they ask where you are from, you don't say from Earth, you say from LA.

Mitchell: Yes. That's true

Paola: So do you think there has to be a one world, kind of, political situation?

Mitchell: Of course that is what has to happen.

Paola: People have some commonality. Right?

Mitchell: In due course, that's what has got to happen. If we survive that long. We might wipe ourselves out before that. I don't think it is a forgone conclusion that we are going to survive. That is where the philosophic, the whole notion of determinism and what the future is like, applies. We are creating the future. It is not determined. If we get our act together and solve our current problems, we could have a sustainable, abundant future. If we don't, we could wipe ourselves out. We are on the verge of doing it with our current politics. It is regressive; going back the other way.

Paola: I need to ask you a personal question. Would you have liked to have had Contact with a cosmic culture?

Mitchell: Yes. Of course!

Paola: This is very ironic because you are the chief astronaut spokesman for the ET presence and have never had contact. [That is] like me, who has been in this work for over 30 years now and has never seen a UFO.

Mitchell: Yes. I would. I would like to speak from first-hand experience instead of second-hand experience.

Paola: Has it been lonely for you to have this vision and not many people to share it with, because the vision you have is kind of a "completion" vision; a kind of overall picture vision, and it is true that you are spending three quarters of your time trying to explain it to people.

Mitchell: I would not put it in those terms because I spend ninety per cent of my time trying to explain it to myself!

Paola: But you know that is truth for you. You are outspoken about that.

Mitchell: Well, I'd like to discover Truth; when I can latch on to something that I think is true. Our knowledge base is incomplete and all we do is keep adding to our knowledge base. I think it laughable, frankly, that the Physics community comes up with a theory for everything. There isn't one theory for everything. There is not one explanation. We may eventually have several theories that can tie things together nicely but there is not a single theory of everything.

Paola: Like the Big Bang being the main theory of creation – and what about Super String theory and others...?

Mitchell: Well, the *Big Bang* has gone away but as far as *Super String*, that is suspicious for me. It all starts out with the notion of *Big Bang*, which starts out, if it were true, starts out with incredibly high temperatures. So they think [we] need to get these high temperatures for this broken symmetry; all this broken symmetry reunited, and we do not have enough energy in the whole galaxy to get to those temperatures, to prove their point. To me, that is the single flaw in Super String theory. Now there are a lot of good points but if it could hold together any better than the *Big Bang* theory, I don't know. I'm not a physicist.

Paola: You are not going in that direction. You are more into the awareness and what you can accomplish as a human. Is that right?

Mitchell: Yes. And I also think we are moving into a direction of quantum cosmology, as opposed to starting with "big bang" and trying to make quantum physics fit into it.

Paola: Quantum Cosmology. That's a new term.

Mitchell: That originates from Quantum processes. That is, the quantum fluctuations within a zero-point field can start the process that builds the process, which builds into matter, an irreversible process. We have some evidence that suggests that. We don't have a Big Bang but we have a lot of little pops! A continuous set of little pops!

Paola: That is a good metaphor. In your talk, one of the things you talked about is that the "intent" creates action. The intent creates our reality, which makes us who we are. If that is true, then that makes us powerful on a planet that has always been undermined by great powers trying to put down the masses. So, is the idea that "intent" creates, and we can create realities, and we can also create events?

Mitchell: We are creating. I don't create yours and you don't create mine but we each create "ours!"

Paola: In the past we have always given up our power to the power structures, so would you agree that it is very likely unpopular to the individual people and that it is hard for them to believe they have power?

Mitchell: You have to tie it with transcendence because, when you transcend the transcendent states, you get past the ego structure, and at that point you don't need laws, you have "morality!" You have inborn, natural ethics because it is built on Love.

Paola: That seems to be the secret word.

Mitchell: Yes. That is why the ancient traditions, even Christianity, say God is Love. There is symmetry here. The fundamental step where you get into this transcendent state is this feeling of ebullience, love and caring and unity.

Paola: And you do not need laws.

Mitchell: That is the law! You learn to live in that. It is hard to live in that too when you are in this world, that is why the great mystics go to the mountains tops; to get away from the world, so they don't have to deal with it – but it doesn't help the world that much."

I do admit that to effect change you need to submit to the "slings and arrows of outrageous fortune" and, especially for a woman researcher, it becomes a severe credibility issue. We all get discouraged at times but to have a conversation like this with Dr. Mitchell was a once-in-a-lifetime event. The metaphysical methodology he speaks about is the very "key" to unlocking the phenomena. This wisdom is that of many centuries of study.

First-hand testimony from those who knew Colonel Corso, as best evidence!

We, here in Rome, knew Colonel Corso very well. He spoke in Pescara, on the Adriatic Coast in 1997 and at the World Symposium in San Marino in 1998. Those present were impressed with his credentials, his honesty and his testimony. He used to ask his skeptics, "Were you there?"

Before I begin to defend Colonel Philip Corso from the outrageous attacks of some American Ufologists, I want to ask the following questions: Why has this man been the object of such controversy? Why debunk the dead who cannot defend themselves? Why go on with this debate, unless it is fueled by economic reasons, since the commonality seems to be the selling of Roswell books? Why put so much energy into this, unless there are ulterior motives? It does not take a genius to figure out that the motives of these debunkers may not be the most "noble." Some of the arguments are ridiculous. We researchers do not base veracity only on documents, especially when dealing with the "black ops world" or with people who had high intelligence clearances. At times there is no paper trail. We all know this. So why allow people who never questioned Colonel Corso themselves, nor knew him, to have the final word on his character?

I have spoken to many major researchers along with Bob and Ryan Wood, who have recently cited *The Dawning of a New Age* Corso manuscript, published in Italian, as a viable resource. They are all puzzled as to why the Corso "bashing." Colonel Philip Corso was very credible. He knew the situation and, at 83-years old, decided to come forward with major disclosure testimony. Corso's motivation was his three grandsons asking for the truth and his belief that it was "time" to tell his story, but only after the death of General Trudeau, as agreed. Colonel Corso told me, as well as his family, that he thought that humanity could handle the truth. We know that many inconsistencies in the book could also be attributed to his co-writer but the core story is true.

Why do these debunkers criticize ex-Minister of Defence, Paul Hellyer, for citing the credibility of the Corso book? We know that, besides calling that "four-star General" to verify Corso's role in Army R&D, the honorable Paul Hellyer must have known "something" of UFOs in the National Security discussions which were obviously part of his position in the Canadian government. So why are these few people still fueling this Corso controversy? Why not speak to the researchers above; most very experienced in their field, and then interview the people who knew him well?

His real story, I find, was told mostly in Italy, where he was on Prime Time television talk show and an honored guest at two conferences. I accompanied him there and spent the week of Easter 1998 with the Colonel and his daughter-in law Liz and his grandsons Andrew and Philip. We had some very revealing conversations. He would talk about conversations he had with Canadian scientist Wilber Smith, and what he called his "German Scientists." These men came from *Operation*

Paperclip, which was launched by the US Government to bring German scientists to the USA in the interest of National Security. Some of them: Wernher von Braun – the "father" of the US space exploration program, Siegfried Knemeyer – the former head of the RLM (Ministry of Aeronautics), Hans Amtmann, Alexander Lippisch, Robert Sarbacher, and others, seem to have been in possession of critical knowledge in the field of aeronautics, space flight and UFO technologies. They came to America in 1946. Some of them worked at Air Material Command (AMC) at Wright Field (later Wright-Patterson) in Ohio. The Colonel had been to Ohio, to the base at Wright Field. At one point in an informal conversation with us in Italy, he said he saw craft there.

Colonel Corso himself reveals all, in his manuscript, his handwritten notes, called *The Dawning of a New Age*. It is a tragedy that it has not been published in English as we have it for sale in Italian in all the book stores. He says, why not invest the time in a "new" scientific approach, that takes us past the paper-pushing and laboratory-experimentation stages of this research and leads us, instead, into a serious discipline, which could include adaptation to an interdimensional phenomena. He suggests the answer was found in time travel and understanding the mystery of space and time.

Some back-engineering projects, according to NSC's (National Security Council staff member and at one time the special assistant to General Trudeau, head of the Pentagon's Foreign Technology Desk) Colonel Philip Corso includes special materials (ceramics, alloys, bio-textiles), lasers, fiber-optics, solid-state electronics, compact discs, supercomputers, biotronic and bio-computer devices, magneto-aero and hydro-dynamics, magneto-gravitation, particle beam weapons, electromagnetic pulse (EMP) engines, stealth technology, night-vision technology, cold fusion, neutronic reactors, etc...

"Give this information to the young people of the world and this country. They want to hear it." Colonel Phillip Corso

Exclusive Interview with Colonel Philip Corso.given Paola Harris and Maurizio Baiata.

Here is an unedited, original interview that Colonel Corso gave to Editor Maurizio Baiata and me, in 1998, in a hotel in Rome. I remember it well!

Colonel Corso: I've just mentioned crop circles, mutilations of animals and abductions of humans. When I was chief of the Foreign Technology Division, I went to the General one day and it was agreed that we would start no projects in the army, in our organization, on those three items: crop circles, mutilations and abductions, but we would watch them. We would keep getting the reports and we would watch them because our main objective in those days was weapons of war. We did it to advance the competitive edge of the Army. Even with the beings, it did not matter to us if they were real or not and it didn't matter if they came by accident or design. Our motive was: if they are real, we are going to be ready. We are not going to sit here like stupid humans and say they are not around. We have to work on the assumptions that they are there and they might be enemies. So I told the General, our main thrust must be that, and I hardly had time to do what I'm doing but I would read the documents, because I could read documents in a minute or so. I said: "I'll keep getting these reports and watch this but we'll do nothing about it, only collect information," and for years I collected documents, at the White House, which talked about mutilations. We knew about them. We made the decision that crop circles were nothing else but integrated circuits. When we'd put in an integrated circuit they'd give us a message. Abductions, we came to the conclusion they're happening but that we were not going to do anything about it. We were receiving materials so I did get two of the implants. There are other implants which I've never talked about, which we knew were real. You could not take them in your hand because they were microscopic, but they were there.

So the future has to go along those lines. When I was working in this field, I know they were real. They happened. I don't think that any other of those people can say this. They weren't cleared. They didn't get the reports. They did not have access to them.

They talk to an abductee and what happens? The critic says, 'hallucination, self hypnotism' and you're finished. How are you going to get past that? Well, if I tell you that the abductee had two implants, it makes it real. You can say, "Colonel Corso told me." It was an area that we never did anything about. We never found out the reason for it because we had our hands full with what we were doing. That wasn't my job to do that. We spent money on the night-viewing device; millions of dollars. That was a product of war. The soldiers of Vietnam could see the enemy at night. Lasers, Fiber Optics, that was the main thrust of our organization. The extraterrestrial himself, I would always say, was the greatest gift they gave us and we did nothing with it. So who was in charge? I was, so that meant I did nothing with it. So in my old age maybe I feel guilty and I have been writing about it now. I realized experts have to come into this and look at this entity, this Being. I know nothing about lungs, the lymphatic system and the body. This Being is, after all, a biological entity. All these stories of clones, that it is against religion; that man wants to live forever, that's all baloney. That clone was made for another purpose: to travel in space. They want to see what space is like. They came here. Without the relationship of the clone with the flying saucer, they never would have made it here.

Paola: Will they attack us?

Colonel Corso: There's no way in the world that I can tell you that they won't attack us but, from a soldier's point of view, I've got to be ready for any attack that might come. If I'm not, I'm negligent and I shouldn't be dressed in a military uniform. You have got to be ready for any eventuality or you'll be destroyed and your country will go with it. If they fight a war we need to realize that their super-intellect is on a different level and I don't think they would fight on our level, with bombs and cannons. Why should they? They could not carry enough bombs and cannons on their space ships to fight us. They might fight us with our bodies, with something that uses no weight, like a type of biological weapon. I think that the super-intellect will fight us on that level. Using bombs and guns is like fighting barbarians. The problem is, those people that think that the scenario is like this are thinking like human beings and not like the aliens. One example is a mistake I made: I had a pen-like artifact I received from the Roswell Crash and it would not go on and I thought the battery was dead so I put it away. See how stupid that was? As if a "Super Race" would use a battery that would wear out in two months! That is ridiculous thinking and yet it happened to me. I am telling you what the British taught me in Intelligence, years ago. Yes, you look for targets and things like that but the main things you look for are "intentions." They were right. You defeat the enemy by knowing his intentions, not by one bomb. It took me guess work to build up the mosaic because I have to think in my own brain, 'What is his intention?' Naturally I'm going to make mistakes because I don't know too much about him, but at least I can try. Whereas this new science could fill in and correct the mistakes I made because of lack of knowledge. And this is what I think it has to come to. I've really never talked like this to anybody, well, maybe with a couple of scientist friends, but usually I don't. My scientists friends are calling me and you know why they are calling me? Because in the book I stated that this extraterrestrial is part of the flying saucer. It is all one. So these are another intelligence. They are ahead of us. They have proven it. One simple reason: they can fly in space and we can't. In the end, the greatest gift was the extraterrestrial, not the hardware.

Colonel Philip Corso, on Videotape, 1997 in Rome, Italy

Monsignor Corrado Balducci
Vatican Representative

Monsignor Corrado Balducci is a close friend. We have spent many hours together discussing current UFO research. Because of our close proximity (living near St. Peter's) in Rome and because we admire each other, we often dine together. Padre Balducci is a pure spirit, whose eyes light up when you discuss extraterrestrial visitations. He is curious, educated and open-minded. He is optimistic and has hope that we will have some kind of celestial "intervention" and be saved from cataclysmic destruction. He sees these visitors as Comic Cultures and he sees them as children of God. He was present at Steven Bassett's X-Conference, for which I served as interpreter, in Washington DC, in 2005, and he was awarded by Bassett for his courage. We both were filmed for the documentary *Fastwalkers* and that last appearance of Monsignor Balducci is historic. He is in his 80s but his words will live on as they represent the unofficial position of the Catholic Church, which has a massive observatory in Arizona and is looking to the skies.

"The city of Mexico is blessed with UFO Sightings. I will continue to be spokesman for the opening up of public opinion and Church attention towards the people from the stars. I will ask the Vatican to dedicate the religious feast day 'Christ, the King of the Universe' to include all its inhabitants!"

Corrado Balducci, Rome, March 2006.

At a conference in Rome in March 2005, organized by Starworks Italia and Area 51 magazine and featuring special guest, Mexican journalist Jaime Maussan, Monsignor Corrado Balducci told the audience that Mexico was blessed with so many sightings because of its incredible openness and faith. Both Jaime Maussan and Monsignor Balducci were awarded the International George Adamski Award at the event in Rome. Mexican Journalist/ Researcher Jaime Maussan explained to the audience that he became interested in the UFO phenomenon after viewing them when they appeared during the last solar eclipse over Mexico.

After seeing all this amazing Mexican film footage, Monsignor Balducci said that the Vatican is very interested in this phenomena and that he was designated spokesman. He told the audience that he had written a note about the importance of his presence at the X-Conference in Washington DC, in 2005, to the current Pope, Benedict the Sixteenth, and that he also knew that the late Pope, John Paul, followed his many TV appearances speaking about UFOs. He added that in the Bible, Jesus is called "King of the Universe" sixty-six times and that in this phrase, it is understood as the "universe and its inhabitants." "There is such a variety of animal and plant species on the planet, do we not assume God would only create one type of life?" added Balducci. "I always wish to be the spokesman for these star peoples, who also are part of God's glory, and I will continue to bring it to the attention of the Holy Mother Church."

"If aliens are visiting us," he adds, "they must be much more evolved because the human species is the lowest rung on the ladder of spiritual development. We have been given discernment and we still fight and kill and are attracted to wrong-doing. If the Church is founded on witness testimony then why can't the governments of the planet believe all the thousands of witnesses who are testimonies to this reality? It is time to speak up and tell the truth!"

NASA and Disclosure

The latest NASA film footage out on DVD is outstanding and indisputable

In Jose Escamilla's documentary film *The Greatest Story Ever Denied,* there is visible proof of unidentified objects in space, artificial structures on the moon and globe-like light spheres around the STS Space Shuttle missions. Those famous intelligent "balls of light", for which I name this book, are now visible. NASA knows and there are those in NASA that wish to tell the truth as well as those who want to maintain the "cover-up"!

Again, in his brilliant speech in Greece, Mr. Côme Carpentier de Gourdon says: "There is now a large number of declassified, or leaked but verified, official reports from various Air Forces, Navies, Armies and international military structures, such as NATO, NORAD et al, about encounters, incidents, chases, dogfights and confrontations with "alien" spacecraft exhibiting properties far superior to any available in the conventional arsenals of earthly powers. For example, there are detailed records about the "Maelstrom missile shutdown" (one among several cases) when, in 1967, visiting UFOs deactivated a number of Montana-based ICBM missiles in their underground silos. A surprisingly high number of military officers of several countries, including 3-star generals, air marshals and admirals, not to mention astronauts in the Apollo program (Russell Schweikart, Brian O'Leary, Buzz Aldrin and Scott Carpenter among others), have admitted publicly to having seen or been shown evidence of UFOs that, in their best judgment, could not have been of human, terrestrial origin."

One such whistleblower is a ground crew astronaut who has been very vocal about his experiences working for 22 years at NASA Kennedy Space Center, Florida. Clark McClelland is currently preparing his own book and I thank him for sharing this material with me. He speaks from first hand knowledge.

Interview with Clark McClelland about his conversation with Senator Barry Goldwater at Kennedy Space Center, July 16ᵗʰ 1969.

Clark C. McClelland, former ScO, Space Shuttle Fleet, Kennedy Space Center, Florida, 1958 to 1992.

Paola: You had several assignments at Kennedy Space Center. That is a beautiful photograph you sent me, of you after the launch of STS-48 shuttle mission. Can you name some of your job titles?

Clark: My titles at the Cape were: Structural Designer, Aerospace Engineer-Mission Planner, Aerospace Engineer- Launch Operations, Technical Assistant to the Apollo Program Manager, Mission Operations Monitor in the LCC (Launch Operations Center).

Paola: Clark, can you name some astronauts that knew of the alien presence and with whom you spoke personally?

Clark: Ellison Onizuka, who saw two, what appeared to be, aliens; Dr. Story Musgrave, *The Demonstration* comments. Comments by Dr. von Braun in *Chasing Juno*, comments in *Interfering with Atlas* and the letter to me from USAF Major Mansmann. Look at my website www.stargate-chronicles.com for these articles and in the *Those Who Know* section for the comments made to me by astronauts Deke Slayton and Gordon Cooper and read what Dr. Edgar Mitchell has said.

Paola: You once told me you talked about UFOs with Senator Barry Goldwater, of Arizona. Can you tell us about it?

Clark: The date July 16th 1969, was the day of the launch of Apollo 11 and the initial kick-off for the first landing of the human race on our neighbor, the Moon. The global importance of this major historic event was very evident at the Kennedy Space Center, Florida. It was Moon Shot Day! Many famous people from all over the world gathered in the VIP launch-viewing area, near the Apollo LCC (Launch Control Center). The security was at its highest level, with VIP guests present from every nation on earth. One guest was a person whom I had supported during his political career: Senator Barry M. Goldwater of Arizona. He had been the Republican Presidential candidate in 1964, running against President Lyndon B. Johnson. He had lost by a wide margin but we, in Florida, had delivered him a victory in Brevard County, Florida and the Space Port area and had pride in ourselves regarding that minor accomplishment. In 1968, Goldwater won back his Senatorial seat in Arizona.

Paola: But Senator Goldwater was also a military man.

Clark: Senator Barry M. Goldwater was a former Major General in the United States Army Air Corp, wanting to be a fighter pilot of a P-47 Thunderbolt and/or a P-51 Mustang aircraft, but was assigned to deliver various aircraft to combat areas. He had flown an estimated 160-plus other planes during his World War II and civilian years. I was also informed that he had been checked-out in an SR-71 Blackbird. That was very impressive to learn.

Paola: So, how was the photo taken?

Clark: During the long countdown of the Saturn V Apollo 11 launch vehicle, I took a breakfast break from the LCC and walked to the nearby VIP guest viewing site, in hopes of meeting Senator Goldwater. As I scanned the numerous people gathered, I asked one of our security guards if he was aware of the location of Goldwater. He pointed his finger to an open field nearby saying, "Do you see that guy over there, setting up his camera tripod, Mac? That's Senator Goldwater." I had my camera around my neck in hopes of having a photo opportunity with the Senator. I strolled across the crabgrass turf, as he was setting up his personal camera. I was surprised he was alone, except for a half dozen other guests that were nearby, also setting up their cameras. I introduced myself and he responded with a polite greeting.

Paola: How did you ask him about UFOs and what did you find out?

Clark: I seriously pondered my next question concerning UFOs and finally asked him if he would discuss the subject with me? I was surprised he had no Secret Service Agents or NASA Public Affairs personnel hovering around him. I explained my position at KSC and my being the NICAP Unit-3 Director for Major Donald E. Keyhoe at KSC. He had met Keyhoe in DC, years before. He approved our discussion on the UFO subject and we began our exchange of information. I began by saying it was obvious he had a deep, abiding interest in UFOs and possible visits of alien races to Earth. He said, "That is accepted fact in Washington, and especially at the Pentagon, young man."

I had some understanding of his alleged statements regarding UFOs in the past and brought up the popular story of his effort to gain entry into a special storage area at Wright-Patterson AFB, which purportedly had alien artifacts in it. He said, "Yes, that's the main event concerning me and UFOs. I was under the impression that a US Senator, with a past as a Major General in the US Army Air Corp and a member of the US Senate Select Committee on Intelligence for many years, would carry some weight in my allowances to enter such an area of military secrecy. I was rudely awakened to reality, very swiftly, when I was denied passage. It had me angry enough to discuss it with a personal friend of mine in the military and I inquired why my position in the US Senate had no such allowance? My friend, General Curtis LeMay, Chairman of the Military Joint Chiefs of Staff at the Pentagon, very angrily told me that I had no need to know. He gave me a lot of hell about my activities at Wright-Patterson. He threatened to end our friendship for life! My God, Mac, that surprised the hell out of me!"

LeMay added, "You stay clear of our mutual friend, "Butch," too (meaning General William "Butch" Blanchard). His having been at Roswell (later Walker) Army Air Base and the 509th, will not gain you any favor for knowledge of that Roswell crash claim, Mac." Goldwater said, "Butch Blanchard was also a very valued friend of mine, since World War II. He was the person who announced that a disc had crashed near Roswell in 1947. This cussing out did awaken me to one fact: that the UFO situation is the highest level of national secrecy. Much higher than the H-Bomb was and more than anything else that is known within the Pentagon, FBI, CIA, DIA, NSA, etc. That is, nothing is higher security than aliens being here on this planet. Then I realized Curtis was correct and I never again approached him on the subject. That seemed to prove to me that UFOs were a fact, and do exist. But, are they all aliens? I highly suspect a majority are! Hell, they are no doubt far ahead of our level of intelligence. The United States Air Force knows the truth, but will they ever reveal it to this nation?"

I quickly said, "Yes, Senator, some UFOs sighted, I have learned through the ONI, are alien." His eyes brightened up and he showed surprise, saying, "Mac, how would you know that as a fact and I was denied the truth?" I said, "Senator, I was here, at KSC, and had also been at Cape Canaveral, since the start of our national space program. With all due respect for your great accomplishments, sir, you were not. I've heard and seen things that, without any doubt, proved to me that UFOs and star races exist."

I said, "Congress is not made aware of secrets of this caliber. The Pentagon controls such disclosures." Goldwater said, "Yes, I get your point. You were, and are, on the cutting edge of technology, Mac. Hell, you have seen events I can only dream about!" I replied, "Yes, sir, more than you know!"

Paola: How much do you think Senator Goldwater really knew?

Clark: I tested the Senator with another question. I asked him if he was, at that time, aware of the fact that several former German scientists were assigned to Wright Field. He said, "No, Mac, I was not." Then one of the nearby launch viewers came close to our location and I stopped the discussion. The man wanted to say hello and shake the hand of Senator Goldwater. Following his departure, I continued, saying, "Those Germans were at Wright since post-World War II and assigned to reverse-engineer certain retrieved hardware that was suspected to be of alien origin. They accomplished that assignment of the object that crashed in Kecksburg, Pennsylvania. It was taken to Wright Field. Senator Goldwater said, "Yes, I recall that incident. What was it? Do you know?" I replied, "Yes, sir, it was a Soviet failed mission to Venus in 1965. It was not alien, Senator. The public was lead to believe it was a UFO. Far easier to explain than a missile from the USSR hitting within the USA." Goldwater agreed.

Goldwater asked if I was aware who the Germans were. I replied, "Yes, one was Siegfried Knemeyer, the former head of the German RLM (The Reichsluftfahrtministerium), the Third Reich's Air Ministry for aircraft development for the Luftwaffe.

He died in 1979, in the USA. Another was Dr. Hans Amtmann, an expert in vertical take-off aircraft. One other I am familiar with is Dr. Alexander Lippisch, who was more well known and a pioneer in tailless aircraft, the US Delta wing fighter, the F-102A Delta Dagger and an advanced design of a ground-effect flying boat. I'm almost certain these men also did a reverse engineering on the object that crashed near Roswell, New Mexico." I could see that what I was telling the Senator may have had his mind in a spin. So, I slowed down.

He continued the conversation saying, "Mac, you work in one of the most secretive and important areas of our national security, on the cutting edge of space science, and are, no doubt, aware of much that has happened and is happening during our missions into space." I confirmed his statement, saying I was also part of an ONI (Office of Naval Intelligence) Unit at Patrick Air Force Base, South of the Cape. He was surprised to hear that fact. He said, "So, you are Naval Intelligence, young man?" I said, "Well, yes sir, but, only one member." He continued, making certain none of the people nearby was within listening distance, "Now, may I ask you what you have heard or seen here?" I joked with him and said, "Do you have a need to know, sir?" and we both laughed.

Paola: This is obvious, Clark. This is the standard phrase! 'The need to know.' Then you took this photo?

Clark: I asked the man if he would take a photo of Goldwater and me together. I asked approval of the Senator and he gave his OK. Following the photo being taken, I thanked both the people. This is the photo I sent you during the launching of Apollo 11; Man's first landing on the moon.

Paola: What kind of conversation did you have about *Operation*

Paperclip and the German scientists? You said you knew some?

Clark: Senator Goldwater asked me, "What's RLM?" I told him it was the German Air Ministry that created the various planes, like the Messerschmitt, Junker, and may have influenced the V-1 and V-2 rockets at Peenemunde. I continued, "Two other Paperclip scientists at Wright Field are Dr. Hans Amtmann and Dr. Alexander Lippisch. I believe all three are still at Wright-Patterson Air Force Base, Senator. Perhaps you can try and contact them there?" The Senator quickly replied, "No, not after that experience with General LeMay, Mac!" I said, "Senator, you are aware of the military rivalry to gain the upper hand over other areas of the United States military, which has been an on-going practice throughout our national history?" He replied, "Yes, I am, having been associated with the military budgets in the Senate." I continued, saying, "There was, and still is, a great rivalry between the US military services and since the USAF and the US Army ABMA were playing the same game between them at Wright Field, the AMC (Air Material Command) Foreign Technology Division of the USAF had captured alien technology and the US Navy wanted it shared with the ONI. Another habitual US Military squabble. Can you imagine the Soviet Union having such squabbles? Not on your life! Admirals and Generals would have been marched to a wall and executed. In fact, Stalin did just that to several of his military officers." Goldwater agreed.

I continued to explain the film, "As we all watched the ONI film, it described the sighting of a huge 400-foot, or larger, saucer-shaped object that was encountered by a US Navy R7V-2 four-engine Constellation aircraft over the Atlantic Ocean. As many as 40 military personnel and air crew observed it as it approached the aircraft and appeared to be observing the Navy plane. It was at an altitude of about nineteen to twenty thousand feet and, at first, the object was mistaken for being a gathering of many ships below the plane, due to its size when initially, and earlier, viewed far below the aircraft by the navigator and commander of the plane." I said, "Senator Goldwater, I cannot recall the names of the flight crew." He said, "Just continue with the incident, Mac. It's very interesting and I was not aware it had happened." I continued, "They all witnessed it and described it as having a large, illuminated outer ring since it, and what some said may have been other craft below, were possibly seen. As the large object approached the plane, at about 1,000 yards, those aboard were mystified and frightened. The crew later said it was a huge, saucer-shaped metallic machine."

Goldwater asked, "Mac, did they show photographs of it in the ONI film?" I told him I was not aware that a film was exposed during the actual incident, so, no, I did not see any depiction of the UFO. If any UFO film, was taken at all, it was apparently under Top Secret classification and not shown in the ONI film. Some comments made by the crew in the film were that they all considered the huge object was "intelligently" controlled. They also said that no living creature, etc., was seen. They added that the craft's speed, from when it climbed from near sea level to their aircraft altitude, was estimated to be about 1,400 to 2,000+ knots, in a brief time lapse of seven to eight seconds.

The Senator said, "That's astounding, Mac! What else was said?" I continued, "The Navy aircraft commander radioed ahead to the Gander Air Force Base control tower and asked if their radar was identifying any other object near his R7V-2. The tower control officer said, "Yes, a larger object and in close proximity to the Navy plane." Sir, they verified that a gigantic craft was on their radar!" He replied, "Mac, I was not aware of that case! I will try and pursue it when I return to Washington." I replied, "Contact Don Keyhoe or Richard Hall, his deputy."

I continued with the sighting saying, "The US Navy Flight Commander was asked by the USAF interviewer at Gander, during their individual and group debriefing, did they see any indication of life? His reply was, "No, but it was intelligently controlled – and my crew and I are all witnesses to that fact!" That object was not remotely controlled; something inside of it was in control! The interrogator would not discuss what the Gander Radar had recorded and refused to allow the Navy to review it. The Navy Commander asked the Air Force Officer, "What is the USAF up to now? You people say UFOs do not exist; what the hell did we see if they don't exist?" The USAF Officer said, "Sorry, we cannot answer any of your questions!"

On 29 May 1998, Barry Goldwater passed away in Phoenix, Arizona. Perhaps he now knows the secrets of that "secret area" at Wright-Patterson Air Force Base and is now aware of other races among the stars.

Several Exopolitical Considerations

It is a new year, 2007, on this beautiful planet, which is burdened with ecological global disaster (the third hottest year recorded) and with the threat of potential destruction by nuclear attacks. The fighting never stops but we are still being watched and being visited.

In the UFO field, two incredible documentaries have surfaced in the United States; one: *Fastwalkers*, which has a spiritual theme and some pretty important researchers, such as Steven Greer, Stanton Friedman and Sgt. Major Robert Dean. But the appearance of Monsignor Balducci is a first, an ante prima. It is part of the unconventional wisdom from extraordinary people seen the world over. He is one of "ours" in Italy.

The second DVD, called *The Greatest Story Ever Denied*, is an editing masterpiece of Jose Escamilla. It contains all the military witnesses involved in the UFO cover-up from the 2002 Disclosure Project, in sound bites. The background music is incredibly beautiful but two things impressed me: the over 2500 hours of uninterrupted live broadcasts and NASA footage from Martyn Stubbs. It includes the voice in the NASA control room actually saying to the astronauts, "We are tracking the alien vehicle." Yes. The alien vehicle!

In the DVD, Colonel Philip Corso is quoted as saying: "Give this information to the young people of the world and this country. They want to hear it! They want it. Give it to them! Don't hide it and tell lies and make stories. They are not stupid!"

The phenomenon is becoming more mainstream with the major sighting at the O'Hare airport reported on November 7th 2006. These were expert witnesses who can recognize airplanes and who hesitated to come forth because of job security but the story hit the mainstream media anyway. It was ironic that a respected journalist like Anderson Cooper on CNN 360 interviewed a O'Hare witness on one hand and immediately included an interview from an editor from the Skeptical Inquirer on the other. This man single handedly debunked Roswell as little pieces of aluminum and balsa wood and the famous Campeche Mexico infra red film as "oil rig flares" moving around the sky. I'm sure the ministry of Defense in Mexico can recognize oil rig flares before they release the film to the world. This is sheer ignorance and is used to discredit the shadowed O'Hare witness almost immediately. We have a ways to go in the disclosure process but the aliens are not waiting.

Lastly, we could see from his words and code of ethics that Colonel Corso was a fine soldier and patriotic man. He was a man of "uncommon wisdom and courage" as were the other expert testimonies in this first section. However, in the next section we will see how back-engineering causes challenges for Exopolitics. The back-engineering of technology confuses the issue in this Exopolitical study and also causes the secret, alien-inspired technology to become the major stumbling block in the *Disclosure* process. The nation possessing this technology rules the world. That is why the secret is kept secret! Alien vehicles do not use gasoline.

The original participants at Steven Bassett's X-Conference in Washington DC
2004

Top: Paola Harris with Richard Hoagland and Dr Robin Falkov, Nexus
conference Abano-Terme Italy.
Front Paola Harris and Webmaster Giovanni Zavarelli
Back :Maurizio Baiata, Pietro Ponzo Laura Tomasi, Pino Morelli, Adriano
forgione

Travis Walton gives Paola an achievement award from **CENTRO UFOLOGICO INTERNATIONALE (CUI) Italy**

Canadian Former minister of Defence Paul Hellyer during the February 2006 interview in Toronto.

I introduced researchers to Monsignore Corrado Balducci: Among them were Dr. John Mack, Steven Bassett, Dr Steven Greer and Jaime Maussan.

Dr. John Mack in one of his last appearances in Florence Italy where he gave *The New World View* Speech to Gruppo Ufologico Academico Scandicci. (GAUS) He affectionately referred to them the "gauzers" because they were a very young group who hold incredible UFO conferences in Florence.

Robert Wood, Dr. Michael Salla, Italian Ufologist and owner of the Roman Restaurant *Lo Zodiaco*, Eufemio del Buono and ***Area 51*** editor Maurizio Baiata at the inauguration of ***Area 51*** magazine in October 2006.

Paola Harris, Esen Sekerkarar, Nick Pope, and CUI director Antonello Lupino on the balcony of my apartment in central Rome.

Memories of Dr. John Mack
Left: Italian editor Hera Magazine, Adriano Forgione, Dr. Mack, Paola Harris, Gildas Bourdais (France)

Dr Dan Burisch with Paola Harris during an interview in Las Vegas where he explains " Looking Glass" technology.

My portrait of Colonel Philip Corso during an Easter spent together in Foligno Italy 1998

Letter to Sicilian Contactee Eugenio Siragusa from Dwight D Eisenhower in 1951.

Al Bielek and Paola Harris, Laughlin UFO Conference in Nevada.

From left to right : Richard Dolan, John Greenwald, Dr Edgar Mitchell- Apollo 14 Astronaut, Steven Bassett, Ann Druffle, Paul Davids, Paola Harris at the Roswell Festival 2005.

Press conference for the Italian version of *The Day After Roswell* in Rome 1997. Paola Harris, Colonel Philip Corso and editor Maurizio Baiata.

Charles Hall with Paola Harris and commercial airlines pilot David Coote. Jerry Pippin interviews Charles Hall and Paola Harris

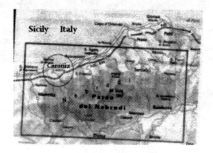

Map of Caronia in Sicily. Site of " fireball"phenomena.

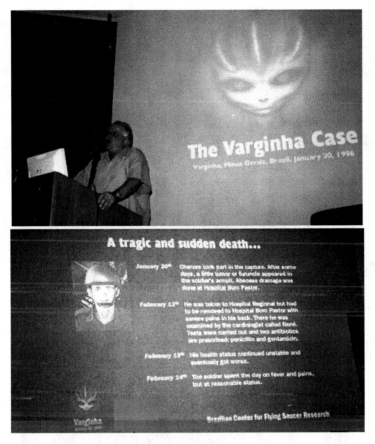

AJ Gevaerd explaining the Varginha case at the Calabria UFO conference in Southern Italy.

Schmidrudi Switzerland. Visit to Billy Meier Semjase Star Center
Carlo Bolla, Guido Moosbruger, Paola Harris, Teresa Barbatelli.

Belgium Psychic Pascal Riolo, Uri Geller and Paola Harris at Uri's Show in Dublin Ireland.

An orb appeared at my *Cosmic Messages* Conference in Riccione, Italy 2006 with top Italian researchers and Native American flute player Danny Many Horses Rael. Many took photos but only this one photographer photographed the orb.

Orb on Dr. Greer's shirt during Cseti Training on Mount Shasta. Pictured from left to right: Linda Willitts, Dr. Steven Greer, Honey Metcalf, Micki Metcalf and Jan Bravo.

Orbs around Rosella in Sardinia. Photo by Pietro
Antique site at Sa Crabarissa Sardinia.

Many orbs with particular signatures in an Antique site at Sa Crabarissa Sardinia.

Clark McClelland and Senator Barry Goldwater at Kennedy Space Center in July 1969.

Paola Harris and Dr J Allen Hynek at NCAR in Boulder Colorado in 1982.
Photo by Russ Crop

Paola Harris speaks at Colorado Briefing on the steps near Denver State Capital organized by Alejandro Rojas in 2006.

Two orbs in this photo are around Al Gore during a book signing for ***An Inconvenient Truth*** at Tattered Cover Bookstore in Denver in the summer of 2006.

Art By Erial www.imaginations window
Paola Harris Extraterrestrial Ambassador

Micki Metcalf calling in Orbs during Cseti training Mount Shasta.
(photo taken by Honey Metcalf)

Adriano Forgione Director of **Hera** Magazine in Italy while standing in an Italian
crop circle. The orb has the face of a child.

Paola Harris and Colonel Philip Corso Monte Mario 1998 in Rome.

Paola Harris and Italian author journalist Giuditta Dembech at the press conference debut of her book on Italy's most famous psychic Rol. There were 40 photos of orbs taken by a single participant.

Betsy McDonald wife of Dr James Mc Donald and Paola Harris at X-Conference 2005

Section Two

Challenges and Protocols
for Future Contact
& The Role of Galactic Diplomacy

Clip from Actor's Studio Interview

Question: Mr Spielberg. You said you hate most when people do not listen. Would you give us some advice as young people who often do not want to listen. What is the importance of listening and lastly, *do you believe in Aliens*?

Answer from Steven Spielberg:

Well, I was taught by my mom and dad that in Judaism the most important prayer is *Hero Israel*, the Lord thy God, the Lord is One and it was taught to me since childhood that the most important thing I could do as a Jew is to " listen" and that was not a way for a parent to say "I know more than you, I'm the boss, you shut up. I'll do all the talking." That was not that way at all. They meant listen to yourself, listen to the little whispers that we tend to not want to hear because they are too soft. We tend to want to listen the shout, not the whisper and so listening carefully is what I was taught all through my life and what I'm just saying is that, when people don't listen, it is not that they don't learn, it is just that they just deny themselves tremendous opportunities and glorious choices. They deny themselves this and it is their own fault.

Yes I do believe in Aliens!

It has been in the last few years that I have moved away from "nuts and bolts" Ufology and the archiving of sightings to a more activist position of gallactic diplomacy and preparing for inevidable "contact" on a political level. I am looking at protocols like the Cseti protocols and political citizen diplomacy efforts like that of Ambassor John MacDonald who spoke at the Hawaii Conference in June 2006 on how to initiate dialogue the way he did for people during the northern Ireland conflict. He said that world governments have their protocols which are not always as successful as citizen diplomacy in getting both sides to sit at the table. Both he and the honorable Paul Hellyer, also present at this meeting, stressed mutual respect for both sides. This process must be organized somehow but we are talking about a near impossibility because these are Cosmic Cultures and we may have little in common.

We are dealing with Cosmic Cultures when we are dealing with aliens. Clifford Stone and Colonel Philip Corso both said there were some fifty different cultures recorded in Pentagon files. They are not only Nordic blondes, or Grey Extraterrestrial Biological Entities(EBE) or Reptilian. There are races that look like us as we will see in the Charles Hall case of the *Tall Whites* on the Nellis Indian Springs base; there are small creatures with reddish brown skin as in the Varginha Brazilian case and there are the *balls of light,* spheres, orbs, fastwalkers or intelligent disembodied entities for which I name this book. There are beings of pure light that do not need bodies.

When we throw these into the mix, it causes us to go into "tilt" mode because we westerners understand nothing which is not concrete. We are conditioned *not* to take this view seriously. Our culture prohibits it. But whether you wish to go there or not, *this phenomena exists on a concrete plane.* Scholars are currently finding this out.

The two examples I wish to use that have influenced my thinking and the title of this book are the case of Pier Luigi Ighina and the case of the evacuation of the village of Caronia on the southern coast of Sicily. These two cases caused me to throw away any preconceived notions of conventional alien visitation. I had no choice but to add new information to my intellectual data bank and though I am discussing it in this book, I still have trouble digesting it as I am not a contactee nor have I had any of this direct contact. But I am seeing that in my reality the images, of these cybernetic disembodied races, are everywhere. They appear as balls of light.

The first example comes from a story I first saw on our 8o'clock Italian Television news about a village in Southern Sicily called Caronia that had a self combusting house phenomena. This phenomena was studied by our scientists and by our military especially the Navy since it was continuous and affected so many people in the village. We wrote an article in our No. 9 issue of June 2006 UFO magazine called Area 51. The article was called "The Village of Fire" because these " balls of Light "came out of what seemed a base in the sea and entered homes, went around the people, the domestic pets, hurt no one but then interacted with the electrical appliances and the houses caught fire. To us this seemed to be an " intelligent" phenomenon.

This phenomenon first began in January 2004, in the province of Messina in Sicily in the town called Marittima di Caronia. In February of that year, the Italian Electric company (ENEL) made a thorough investigation of the voltage boxes and decided to shut down the electricity. The problem was that the phenomena still continued with new fires and burning wires even without the electrical feed. How can this happen without electrical energy to fuel this combustion? Even the sofas and couches were catching fire in the homes. All this was happening in front of the ENEL technicians and townspeople so on February 9th the Italian Civil Defense force proclaimed that zone off limits and cordoned it off. Surveillance cameras were placed there and, for its own protection, the whole town was evacuated. All this caused the fires to stop, but that zone is still under surveillance. Some interesting explanations have been that it was a volcanic or geo-thermic phenomena but most scientists disagree because it is such a isolated case. To add to this mystery, some fisherman reported a " boiling effect in the water as they saw balls of green light exiting from the sea and some reported sightings of unidentified flying objects. Several citizens saw these spheres in their homes but they did not experience any burns nor illness as their electric appliances caught fire. If this is a mystery connected to the UFO phenomena, we know there must be some secret investigation going on somewhere.

There are some who are blaming the infamous project HAARP and connect it to a microwave attack. They claim that the town is an experiment of the " dark Forces" that direct these HAARP weather alteration experiments.

All in all there were two elements that struck me, one that these balls of light avoided hurting the inhabitants as they shot around the houses and secondly, they seemed to rise out of the water. What kind of civilization is this? How do you deal with this? How do you communicate with it? I did ask a military advisor about Caronia and he simply said "If this UFO hypothesis were to be true, we are terrified because we can do little except to protect the people. Furthermore we would truly feel helpless as if our hands were tied. What would we do? Attack them? With what? "

I could see his frustration but it brought home to me the fact that humanity needs to deal with it and not ignore it. We need to have some protocols in place; we need to discuss it.; we need to have clarity and openness and the countries of the world need to share research on a planetary level because it may be happening somewhere else. *Balls of light*, whether they be filmed by NASA around the Tether that broke in space as seen in the Escamilla documentary, or are *orbs* around the STS missions, or whether they are *light balls* coming out of the Adriatic Sea in the 70's as in the case of the Pescara phenomena as reported by Italian Fishermen in Italy or whether they appear as *orange orbs* over

Phoenix during the Phoenix lights on March 13,1997 as described and filmed by Dr. Lynne Kiteii; All this needs to be studied and added to current UFO research.

So I am suggesting those orbs that appear in the "infrared film" taken in Mexico and perhaps those that show up with particular characteristics on digital photos need to be dealt with. All kinds of spheres of light and also *signature orbs* are a new reality and may be under intelligent control if they themselves are not intelligences. The one clear *orb* which has a definite signature pattern on my cover was taken by Barb McCombs in Avesbury, England which is considered "crop circle" country and the one with the child's face on my photo section was taken by Pino Morelli in a crop circle in Italy this year. The appearance in photos of particular orbs in movement with a particular signature needs to be studied. Particles of dust and moisture do not intelligently move up and around rooms, fields and often around certain people like the one on Steven Greer's chest as seen in the Photo section. There is some message here, some opening, some new discovery that in future years will be seen as common place when humanity trains its eyes to the infrared spectrum. It is just the beginning.

Like the expert Mexican researcher journalist Jaime Maussan who is still receiving astounding film footage of flotillas of orbs flying under intelligent control over Mexico City, I predict that with the proper awareness and serious study, these light spheres will become the focus of future UFO research. They may not be conventional craft but they are still to be taken seriously and I wish to open the door to that possibility with this book. If you do not think it affects mankind, then ask those one hundred and forty people who were asked to leave their homes in Caronia, Sicily What remains there are surveillance cameras. Ironically we are watching "those" who are watching us.

The second incident that brought my attention to *light beings* happened in 2003. It was then that I made a trip up to Imola Italy with a friend Illario Pierpaoli. Imola is famous for its Ferrari car racing.

But Imola is also where a ninety-year old collaborator of Guglierlmo Marconi named Pier luigi Ighina had his laboratory. In Italy, he is known as a scientist who "came from the stars". In Italian scientific research, he was the genius that, in only sixteen years, discovered what he called "the magnetic atom". It is said that he was Marconi's cosmic and spiritual guide at the time when he and Marconi worked on secret projects together that were hidden from conventional scientific channels.

His inventions, which influence as well as interact with the electro-magnetic field around every living thing, are renowned in Italy. He has created special antennas that can cure disease, dissipate clouds and cause natural phenomena to happen. He had registered patents for all these devises plus he has written a book in Italian about the magnetic atom called " L'atomo magnetico. Ighina was a charismatic old man, already in his nineties when I interviewed him and perfectly lucid with a head of beautiful white hair. I am glad that I met him before he passed away two years ago because he shocked me out of my complacency.

When I arrived in his three room rustic laboratory in the country, the first thing that struck me as I walked in were the colorful portraits of beautiful beings of light which were hung very high on the walls. They had an Indian style to them as their clothing resembled Mandelas of colored lights. Instead of looking at the many inventions on his wooden workbench, I asked Igina, "who are those people? Did you live in India? He answered that those were the " space brothers" that had "downloaded him and Guglielmo Marconi with these inventions and the information about the workings of the universe. At the time I did not know that Tesla claimed to have a very similar heritage, that he had similar claims and was constantly persecuted by conventional science and government intelligence agencies. These geniuses had all been contemporaries.

So space brothers are downloading scientists and for what reason? According to Igina, it was a warning that the Earth was in its final death throws due to a dying ecology and a lack of spiritual concern from its inhabitants. "We are in auto-destruction mode and these light beings were warning us,"he said. So what I surmised was that the information given to Ighina was that electromagnetism and solar energy (since many of his inventions had solar collectors attached to a generator which I imagined was for magnification) was the salvation of mankind. These devices cured all types of diseases and provided new sources of energy from nature itself. Well, I thought of the fact that this planet is run economically by the transnational companies, and oil, banking and pharmaceutical conglomerates. They are the very foundation of our society and ironically the very cause of our ruin. The masses are kept under control, live in "consumer mode" and to think that Pier Luigi Ighina believed the key to our salvation was nature, the sun, and its solar energy.

There were many testimonials of Ighina's genius and Ighina's success in Italy. He is called "the cosmic scientist" and he told me personally that sometimes on a hillside he spoke to these people, these light beings who were more inter-dimensional than interplanetary. There is *a thought*. Not all aliens come from our galaxy nor from other planets but exist on different planes of reality. Are there not eleven dimensions now accepted by modern theoretical physicists? I had to face that not only were there aliens without bodies but those who are downloading scientists with earth-shattering information. I later learned that there is a Marconi tower in England close to where one of the crop circles appeared and that some of Marconi's work was financed by the Vatican. There is much investigation still to do that could give us some answers. That year, I spoke in Naples in a book store and one of Marconi's close relatives and it might have been his granddaughter was in the audience and she approached me and whispered in my ear that she needed to speak to me. She simply told me that I was on the right track and aliens exist. I have been trying to contact her ever since but she is not responding. I can understand because the theory that many of our scientific discoveries came from the stars would be revolutionary and very controversial in our closed minded society. On the other hand, I am convinced this is a fact based on the testimony of Pier Luigi Ighina and the books about Nicola Tesla and some confidential conversations I have had with several scientists who are my friends.

In the United States, controversial theoretical physicist Jack Sarfatti who lives in San Francisco maintains, that as a teenager, he received several cryptic-phone calls from a robotic computerized voice aboard a space ship saying he would meet other scientists like him in twenty years and ironically he became was part of a gifted program created by Walter Breen called Starfleet Academy. But then Breen is supposedly the creator of MENSA, the association used to identify genius level people. Sarfatti adds that in 1953,in Brooklyn New York, there was a Jr. American Rocket Society Basement Laboratory near Brooklyn College, Flatbus; that Walter Breen's Super kids were influenced by Dr. William Sheldon, Eugene McDermott, Arthur Young, Andrija Puharich and L Ron Hubbard's "Round Table" with links to "Sandia" in New Mexico. Read Sarfatti's book *Destiny Matrix* for whole story and begin to connect a " few dots"! These names are impressive movers and shapers of our current modern some times " new age" discoveries and cosmic thinking but they are also linked to the esoteric philosophies like scientology. All this sounds like a Roddenberry science fiction script from *Star Trek.*

From the Phyllis Schlemmer's book *The Only planet Of Choice,* we know that, on at least one occasion, Gene Roddenberry asked questions of Tom, spokesman for the Cybernetic council of 9 disembodied entities whom Schlemmer channeled. According to the book The *Stargate Conspiracy*, this group of alien entities became the inspiration for the "New Age" practices including some of the SRI Psi scientific research with Israeli psychic Uri Geller. We can see a "ball of light" connection with his story. When Uri as a young child of five, he was supposedly beamed in the forehead by a light being who activated those metal-bending powers. In Israel recently there seems to be a witness to that event who says he followed this ball of light to Uri's apartment and it went right through the door. After all these years, we seem to be peeling off the layers of the onion perhaps getting to some *truth*. Uri is very connected to *Remote Viewing* and psychic experiments of the 70's at SRI, and also with the UFO phenomena as he photographed several UFOs when he was young. He, like Spielberg in the Actor's studio interview, has publicly stated that he firmly believes in aliens. When hypnotized by Andrija Pulharich, it seems Uri has a relationship to a super computer called *Spectra* aboard a space ship. Uri Geller has not only become a planetary phenomenon but as a friend, I know him as a regular guy who has a regular family.

It is interesting that Uri on his website is pictured with American Senators; Senator Pete Domenici, Former Senator Alan Cranston CA)(deceased), Senator Fritz Hollings (So. Carolina). and in another occasion Uri is pictured with Vice President Al Gore, Yuli M. Vorontsov, First Deputy Foreign Minister of the Soviet Union and Anthony Lake (then National Security advisor, later head of the CIA), and Senator Claiborne Pell, Chairman of the US Senate Foreign Relations Committee. Uri's task was to mentally bombard Yuli Vorontsov and the group at the Nuclear Arms Reduction Treaty Negotiations in Geneva, Switzerland, to sign the nuclear treaty, which they did. So we can surmise that the once light-beamed Uri Geller is involved in these political peace-making efforts using the only communication method we have to talk to alien cultures, balls of light, or disembodied entities and so on and so forth, and that is mental telepathy.

Another interesting fact is that Jack Sarfatti states that it was he who introduced Uri Geller to Steven Spielberg and by *connecting the dots*, I can see where the 70's paranormal research, and revolutionary discoveries are the key to this puzzle of "alien intervention"! There were some interesting conversations going on with some major top players in Hollywood, some interesting films emerged from this. Science fiction, served by the Hollywood film industry has provided a bridge to the general public, to spread awareness, test reactions and manipulate information by passing some factual data as fantasy to entertain the masses. Speaking about *Close Encounters of the Third Kind*, Steven Spielberg is quoted as saying" *I really found my faith when I learned that the government was OPPOSED to the film. If NASA took the time to write me a twenty-page letter, then I knew there must be something happening.*"

The first movie to receive government approval was *The Day the Earth Stood Still*! It warned that earthlings must become peaceful or else be quarantined. Then came " *Close Encounters of the Third kind* (a term coined by the Dr. Hynek himself)which came out in 1978 and tested the public reaction to the hundreds of sightings world wide. The contact scenario or alien abduction scenario was then studied by the late Dr. John Mack, a Harvard University professor, who wrote the book *Abductions*. He was one of many with Bud Hopkins and David Jacobs. He found that these people believed they were telling the truth about their contact experience. On a subconscious level, planetary disclosure in the 70's was creeping into our reality and either the governments were guiding it or they were threatened by it. I am guessing it was a little bit of both.

But we return to two elements that are the theme of this book; cybernetic beings sometimes called artificial intelligence and balls of light, not your conventional " alien" profiles. Both have to do with the stories above. If you wish to complicate the picture and throw the work of Philip K Dick into the mix, then it gets very complex because we are questioning our reality in regards to the existence of *Time travel*. I cannot exclude this as Sarfatti mentions it in the case of his formulas in theoretical physics with the component of consciousness. He, as well as I, believe this phenomena is connected with time-travel and the awareness of synchronicities all described in concept of Valis (Vast Active Living Intelligence System) created by Science Fiction writer Philip K Dick who talks of cybernetic super computers. As we know Philip Dick wrote the story line for the popular films *Bladerunner, Minority Report* and *Paycheck*. It is said that he, like Andrija Pulhariach, was somewhat involved with the Intelligence community, and was one of those 70's players. Jack Sarfatti really identifies with his work.

Is this synchronistic principle evidence of Philip K Dick's Valis and Jack Sarfatti's super-cosmos principle at work? Phillip K Dick says in VALIS that "We are not individuals. We are stations in the single mind" also that "Space and Time were revealed as mere mechanisms of separation". Philip Dick has written that *Valis* showed him the "Golden Section," the Fibonacci series of numbers, the law of similarities. Recalling that I'd read on Sarfatti Science Seminar that Philip Dick was on record as having said VALIS was at work in the [non-local] cause and effecting of events taking place during WWII, and also he said that VALIS showed him the G.S. and Fibonacci series, in that light this. The Golden Section (G.S.) world-line seems not only an example of an historical irony, but much more than that, it serves to show an appropriate preferred irony. "Non-locality" is the current scientific explanation for all matter being connected and consciousness being part of that matter whether it be a neutron stimulated in one part of the world which reacts in a laboratory somewhere else or human minds being affected by far away events. Former SRI Physicist Russell Targ explains that "this is responsible for our honed telepathic ability and our ability to see into a " possible future and the synchronicities that may result". Einstein once termed the distinction between past, present and future "a stubborn illusion". So where does it leave us poor humans in our understanding of our true reality and in particular the UfO Phenomena?

On a personal level, synchronistic irony is what leads me into this research after I saw the film *Close Encounters of the Third Kind* and with my Hynek connection. It lead me on the path to the research I am doing today, although I would have preferred a phone call from a "supercomputer" aboard a space ship a-la-Jack Sarfatti.

From the following paper on time travel, I think I need to present the following concepts which are but theories. I need to present this before I go into the interview I did with Al Bielek. He claims that he took part in the famous *Philadelphia Experiment* which he says opened a *dimensional porthole* that let in diverse alien races. The *Time Travel* concept cannot be excluded from our research nor from this book. In a brilliant article by Dennis Overbye, (N Y Times Staff Writer, Tuesday, June 28, 2005) entitled *Time Travel: Remembrance of Things Future: The Mystery of Time Travel*, he says that famed gravitational physicist Dr.Kip Thorne of Cal Tech postulates that wormholes [Einstein-Rosen bridges] can be used as a sort of "Galactic subway" for time travel by threading together wormholes with the Casimir energy thereby keeping them apart and from collapsing. Thorne's theory was used in the Carl Sagan inspired movie *Contact* for Jodie Foster's faster-than-light travel across the galaxy using these wormholes. Dr. J Richard Gott, author of the 2001 book *Time Travel in Einstein's Universe: The Physical Possibilities of Travel Through Time*, is one of a small breed of physicists who spend part of their time (and their research grants) thinking about wormholes in space, warp drives and other cosmic constructions, that "absurdly advanced civilizations" might use to travel through time." If general relativity, Einstein's theory of gravity and space-time is true, it allows for the ability to go back in time and kill your grandfather, The article adds, "when it comes to the nature of time, physicists are pretty much at as much of a loss as the rest of us who seem hopelessly swept along in its current. The mystery of time is connected with some of the thorniest questions in physics, as well as in philosophy, like why we remember the past but not the future".

Jack Sarfatti, in one of his many e-mails to his Sarfatti Physics Seminar groups, added this research data. "It was nearly two decades ago when science fiction media (TV, film and novels) began to adopt traversable wormholes, and more recently *star gates*, for interstellar travel schemes that allowed their heroes and heroines to travel throughout our galaxy. Little did anyone outside of relativity physics know but that in 1985 physicists M. Morris and K. Thorne at CalTech had in fact discovered the principle of traversable wormholes right out of Einstein's *General Theory of Relativity* (GTR, published in 1915). Morris and Thorne (1988) and Morris, Thorne and Yurtsever (1988) did this as an academic exercise, and in the form of problems for a physics final exam, at the request of Carl Sagan who had then completed the draft of his novel Contact. Sagan wanted to follow the genre of what we call science "faction," whereby the story's plot would rely on cutting-edge physics concepts to make it more realistic and technically plausible. This little exercise ended up becoming one of the greatest cottage industries in general relativity research – the study of traversable wormholes and time machines. Wormholes are hyperspace tunnels through *space-time* connecting together either remote regions within our universe or two different universes; they even connect together different dimensions and different times. Space travelers would enter one side of the tunnel and exit out the other, passing through the throat along the way. "

This concept of time-travel and the discussion of the Philadelphia experiment always came up in our conversations with Colonel Corso author of *The Day After Roswell*. I was always curious about this so when I happened to run into Al Bielek at the Laughlin UFO Congress, I had my own questions to ask. This is the text of what he said. It connects to the discussion of dimensional portholes and opening up of a dimension to cause the visits of several ET craft and maybe *balls of light* craft. The idea of transporting consciousness from one physical body to another, as Al Bielek claims happen to him, is very controversial but worth the study. It is also interesting to me that he says Tesla coils were used and Einstein's consulting was part of the experiment. This becomes one of our future challenges in Ufology: to understand Time and Time Travel, "fast maneuvering" craft or *Fastwalkers* and maybe to design a " New Physics" to accommodate this new reality!

The Philadelphia Experiment and Time Travel

Interview with Al Bielek
www.philadelphia-experiment.com
March 2005 Laughlin, Nevada

Paola: What was the Montauk Project?

Bielek: That was a project that appeared between 1975 and 1983. It collapsed and was resurrected in 1987. It was run by the German scientists who came over under *Operation Paperclip*. They worked for twenty years at Brookhaven National Laboratories and they were kicked out of there about 1967.While looking for a new home, they heard about Montauk and the projects out there and they went out there. At that time it was still operated by the US. Military Air Force. They were doing the research for [the] SAGE radar project: Over-the-Horizon radar (OTH). When they got through with the testing and they were in the process of shutting them down, the German scientists heard about it. The German scientists said, "We would like to do some further research. We'd like to show you how to do things, like win the next war by pushing a button." The military were very interested. So the scientists came in and the Military packed up and left and they were there from 1968 until 1983, when it collapsed and was resurrected for a few years in 1987 by the same German scientists, until the Air Force took it over 1991. In taking it, the Air Force was concerned with the Hale-Bop Comet problem. They knew about it before Dr Hale and Dr Bop ever knew about it and they were doing the work to defect it, which they did do, successfully. The Air Force project – "Project Sky Pebbles" was the official name – closed down in 1998 and the Navy came in and took over about the summer of 1998 and they are there still, in the underground. They cleaned off almost all of the old buildings, with the exception of the radar tower, and cleaned it up and it is a park now. So Montauk Point, on the surface, is a park. Underground, it is still a military base, being used for the Navy, and nobody knows for what and nobody that I know of, at this point, has any knowledge of what they were doing and why they are there at the present time. A group of civilians are working for them and have their own separate housing village.

Paola: The Montauk Project has to do with time travel, right?

Bielek: It had to do with *time travel* and mind control. The Montauk boys came out of there originally and they were moved off that base to another area down under, all connected with every major city in the US and major cities in Europe.

Paola: You know I need to ask you this because I have to. How are you privy to this information? How do you know?

Bielek: Because I was part of it. I was part of the Montauk Project and I was a major part of the Philadelphia Experiment. I worked for the Montauk Project for a number of years. I was a civilian. Originally, they put in the SAGE system: 28 radar towers around the periphery of the US and, as they went to the next phase, which was a higher-powered system (Bemus Project), they could pick up a missile launched in Russia as it left the ground. The tower on Long Island remained completely operative after the Military pulled out and the Germans took it over to build their own systems. It was also done in conjunction with a group of aliens that the US government said would be part of the project to develop the time tunnel. We knew how to do *time travel* at that point but we did not know how to make a wormhole.

Paola: What year was this?

Bielek: Montauk became operational under the German control approximately in 1970 and became effective about 1976 until 1983.

Paola: I have to ask about the alien involvement. Do you know about the alien involvement or were you involved with the aliens?

Bielek: Montauk Point was called that because originally the Montauk Indians were there. They were kicked out by the US government about 1900. The Pyramids were torn down. I understand there were pyramids there. I understand that there are some people on the island who have pictures of it, but I have not seen it myself.

Paola: Have you seen the aliens?

Bielek: Yes, at Montauk.

Paola: What were they? The human-type aliens?

Bielek: No. They were a mixture of the human-type as well as some others from all over, including a Draco, who was in charge of some others.

Paola: A Draco; is that a Reptilian type?

Bielek: A particular species of alien who stands 7 feet tall. Some are winged; some are not. They are very heavy, about 450 pounds. They are very intelligent and the one who was there was in charge of other aliens. They had appeared on the Eldridge deck in 1943, when we ripped a hole through the fabric of space-time and became part of the collaboration on time travel technology. They said, "We can show you how to create this wormhole."

Paola: Are you saying aliens were involved with building time travel technology? In what way?

Bielek: You can do that simultaneously. You can build the equipment;

95

you can do that. "We will show you what to build and how to build it."

Paola: What would be the benefit of their teaching us how to build time travel equipment? What would be the benefit for them? What would they get out of it?

Bielek: What they got out of it was that they told the government that: "We have our agenda. We wish to use the station when it is working properly. We wish to use it for our own agenda." The government agreed with that. What "our own agenda" was happened on August12th, 1983, when they locked up with the Eldridge, or the ship they called *the Eldridge* and, on August 12ᵗʰ, 1943, they threw a hole in space-time, forty-years wide, in which to let their own large ships through, because their ships were in a war with somebody else and they wanted to get through to this Universe.

Paola: So was it like tearing a hole in a dimension to let them through. Is that part of the Philadelphia experiment or is it a spin off? Did they know they were going to do that?

Bielek: They knew they were going to do that and they did it deliberately because they delayed the second test for the Philadelphia Experiment until 12 August 1943. It had to be on the 12 August because the Earth has its own biorhythms – like the human biorhythms. They all peak out, like the Earth biorhythms peak out, all four of them. The Earth's peak out on the 12 August every twenty years, plus or minus half a day. That is, [the years] 1943, 1963, 1983, 2003, 2023 have a synchronizing effect on certain affairs and certain matters. In the case of 12 August 1983, we were conducting experiments; they were conducting the Montauk experiment. The two experiments synchronized and locked in. That was done very deliberately, not only to pull the Eldridge into Hyperspace, but in order to produce a sort of wormhole effect – to actually [cause] a breach in space-time large enough for the aliens' ships to get through.

Paola: OK. You said "alien ships" plural, so there are different alien ships and brands of aliens who want to get through that hole?

Bielek: They could.

Paola: You don't know which ones came through? You don't know who was at war?

Bielek: I do not know. Possibly the government knew.

Paola: And this information came through to you as you supposedly were part of that project?

Bielek: Yes. We found out some of the missing links afterwards. We jumped off the ship; we wound up in 1983, on the territory of Montauk, and we were taken in to meet John von Neumann and some of the other people and they told us quite a bit of what was going on. They, themselves, did not [know about] the alien connection causing the breech in space-time but they knew the two experiments had locked up. Von Neumann told us that so we had to go back to the ship and destroy the equipment so the ship would return to its original starting point. We said, "We don't know how we got here; how can you send us to the decks of the Eldridge?" They said, "No problem! We can take control over space-time. We can send you anyplace we want."

Paola: The government said this?

Bielek: No. John von Neumann said that. They did; they sent us through the wormhole to the decks of the Eldridge.

Paola: They sent you through the wormhole?

Bielek: Myself and Duncan.

Paola: How does that feel? Is that just being here one minute and gone the next…?

Bielek: Well, we knew we were being propelled through something. There a slight feeling when you are going through space-time. The first trip you make can be quite nauseating and after that you sort of get used to it.

Paola: You got dizzy and nauseated and that kind of thing? It is like traveling?

Bielek: Well, we knew we were being propelled through something. There is a slight feeling when you go through a wormhole. We were a little nauseated, not like the first time, but, in any case, we went back and we destroyed the equipment as directed and the ship returned to 1943 and we then saw the problem of the sailors buried in the steel deck and the bulkhead. Duncan took one look at this and he headed for the railing, jumped over and disappeared – and went back to Montauk in the 1980s and worked there and had some problems himself. But that was in the records we read later. After passage of normal time and Duncan no longer there, I became part of the Montauk Project at a later date. Much later, after they changed my identity from Ed Cameron to Al Bielek, because I was there on Montauk as Al Bielek.

Paola: In other words Al Bielek was Ted Cameron. Would not it be the other way around?

Bielek: They are both the same person. Except, in 1953, the Navy got tired of me and wanted to find some way of getting rid of me without killing me, because they knew it would cause enormous reactions and problems in terms of space-time; because they were afraid I had traveled so much in time that there would be a collapse in the space-time continuum in the period where I had been and I had gone through, so they decided they couldn't do that. So they cooked up a plot to age-regress me; whitewash all my memories. [They regressed me to a] nine-month old kid and sent me back to another family in the past, to 1927, which were the Bieleks and those were the only parents I knew for many other years.

Paola: That is amazing! With this time travel thing, what would you say was the time, the dates that the government was working with time travel?

Bielek: 1938.

Paola: With the Nazis, right?

Bielek: The Nazi's were working on it also but they never completely solved the problems. They solved the rest of them after they had been extracted from Germany, at the end of World War II, and brought to the United States under Operation Paperclip.

Paola: Those *Paperclip* guys did a lot of things, but Colonel Philip Corso had the feeling that the aliens at Roswell were from the future, coming back to warn us about nuclear power, and he believed that they were time travelers. He told me, "Paola, we have discovered a *Time Machine!*" But I never knew what he was talking about. But he did bring us material on the Philadelphia Experiment. Is there an occasion when somebody has changed the time-space continuum that you know of and history has changed?

Bielek: Yes.

Paola: Where would that be?

Bielek: I can think of two specific items. Number one: History says that the South lost the Civil War and they didn't; they won it! It was changed later, by the use of the Montauk Project, or a different one, I am not sure. But they went back and changed history deliberately because I run into people who remember the fact that the South won the Civil War and some of the earlier textbooks said that; the Southerners believed that, even when I was in high school. The second thing that turned up is – how well do you remembering the era of the German Nazis, the Swastika? Which way did it point at the top? Which way did it appear to be rotating in your memory?

Paola: The right?

Bielek: It always used to point to the left. That was the Nazi symbol for years. It was a sacred symbol which they took from certain Indians and, of course, those tribes do not like that happening. They objected violently. It was adopted by the Nazi hierarchy and pointed to left. Now it points to the right and I saw it happen on TV and I could not believe what I was seeing, because it always pointed to left and suddenly it was pointing to the right. The textbooks have changed, and the monuments, or anything that showed the Nazi swastika, suddenly it is all pointing to the right. It changes everything, even symbolically.

Paola: Colonel Corso said that certain events in time have been changed and we are in an altered timeline.

Bielek: We operate and live on, what you might call, a timeline. The time field is actually a closed loop; it is a gigantic loop. If you go far enough forward in time, you will wind up crossing over and going into the past because it is a connecting link, so to speak, and it is a huge loop. I cannot describe it as something physically in space, but in terms of time, it is a huge loop. I do

100

not know how many years are involved in it, but eventually you will come to the cross-over, plus or minus the infinity point, as it is called, and you are in the past, the very ancient past in the galactic history and, if you keep going forward, you will eventually come up to our present time. It can be navigated with the proper time-travel equipment. You can go forward or backwards. Some scientists today say maybe time travel forward is possible but it is not possible in reverse. That is absolute nonsense! If you look at the equations correctly, you will see that you can go either way.

Paola: You Can go either way. What I asked you specifically though instead of just the swastika., is there an occasion like the death of Kennedy where he was alive and he didn't get killed or of some person being here who should not be here

Bielek: Specifically, no. I think it happened.

Paola: What Colonel Corso said is: "They came once, in the Roswell incident."

Bielek: There were two ships involved and the other disappeared, due to the radar system we had developed that was interfering with their navigation system.

Paola: But Corso said that he saw the ship ten years later, in 1957, in "Red Canyon", in an encounter. What benefit is it for us to have time travel technology?

Bielek: That is a very good question. I don't know as it has any real benefit.

Paola: It must, or they would not do it!

Bielek: It is a toy to certain government groups because they can use it to travel through time and change history. That is the principal reason it has been used. Of course, other travelers from the future have come into our time and in particular, *The Wingmakers*, out of the twenty-eighth century, and they have contributed some technology.

The premise is that a race of robots will come to the earth to take it over (the M51 group). Basically, if they, he scientists can take that point in time in which they, the robotic race are about to discover the Earth and cloak the earth, as such, then the ship goes on by and doesn't see it

They also are experimenting with sound, as in the movie *Stargate*. All of that music was synthesized in a computer. No human voice, no real instruments; they even replicated a 36-foot-diameter, vast base drum, which does not exist now. I do not know if they have one in the future. All this was sent back and sent to the producers.

Paola: You said the benefit was to change history, but would it not be beneficial to tear another hole in space and create another situation that would benefit the aliens? Don't they come through and travel through wormholes that go to other realities?

Bielek: That is possible. If the aliens were to come in and were knowledgeable about space-time, yes, they could rearrange some of our history for us that would make it more advantageous for themselves I do not know which aliens have time travel technologies but I know the Pleiadians do. We created wormholes with Montauk but the Ancients already had wormholes, called 'Stargates.' This is all possible.

TIMELINE on TIME TRAVEL

Details from the new website for Al Bielek

The story begins in June of 1943, with the U.S.S. Eldridge, DE

(Destroyer Escort) 173, being fitted with tons of experimental electronic equipment. This included (according to one source):

- two massive generators of 75 KVA each, mounted where the forward gun turret would have been, distributing their power through four magnetic coils mounted on the deck
- three RF transmitters (2 megawatt CW each, mounted on the deck)
- three thousand '6L6' power amplifier tubes (used to drive the field coils of the two generators)
- special synchronizing and modulation circuits
- a host of other specialized hardware

These were employed to generate massive electromagnetic fields which, when properly configured, would be able to bend light and radio waves around the ship, thus making it invisible to enemy observers.

The *Experiment*, said to have taken place at the Philadelphia Naval Yard and also at sea, took place on at least one occasion while in full view of the Merchant Marine ship S.S. Andrew Furuseth and other observation ships. The Andrew Furuseth becomes significant because one of its crewmen is the source of most of the original material making up the PX legend. Carlos Allende, a.k.a. Carl Allen, wrote a series of strange letters to one Dr Morris K. Jessup, in the 1950s, in which he described what he claims to have witnessed: at least one of the several phases of the Philadelphia Experiment. At 0900 hours, on 22 July 1943, so the story goes, the power to the generators was turned on, and the massive electromagnetic fields started to build up. A greenish fog was seen to slowly envelop the ship, concealing it from view. Then the fog itself is said to have disappeared, taking the Eldridge with it; leaving only undisturbed water where the ship had been anchored only moments before. The elite officers of the Navy and scientists involved gazed in awe at their greatest achievement: the ship and crew were not only radar invisible but invisible to the eye as well! Everything worked as planned, and about fifteen minutes later they ordered the men to shut down the generators. The greenish fog slowly reappeared and the Eldridge began to dematerialize as the fog subsided, but it was evident to all that something had gone wrong. When boarded by personnel from shore, the crew above deck was found to be disoriented and nauseous. The Navy removed the crew and, shortly after, obtained another.

In the end, the Navy decided that they only wanted radar invisibility, and the equipment was altered. On the 28 of October 1943, at 17:15, the final test on the Eldridge was performed. The electromagnetic field generators were turned on again, and the Eldridge became near-invisible; only a faint outline of the hull remained visible in the water. Everything was fine for the first few seconds and then, in a blinding blue flash, the ship completely vanished. Within seconds it reappeared, miles away, in Norfolk, Virginia, and was seen for several minutes. The Eldridge then disappeared from Norfolk, as mysteriously as it had arrived, and reappeared back in Philadelphia Naval Yard. This time, most of the sailors were violently sick. Some of the crew were simply missing, never to return.

Some went crazy, but, strangest of all, five men were fused to the metal in the ship's structure. The men that survived were never the same again. Those that lived were discharged as 'mentally unfit' for duty, regardless of their true condition. So, what had begun as an experiment in electronic camouflage, ended up as an accidental teleportation of an entire ship and crew, to a distant location and back again, all in a matter of minutes! Although the above may seem fantastic, one must remember, that in the 1940s the atomic bomb was also being invented.

TIMELINE for Ed Cameron-Al Bielek

1916: Birth date for Ed Cameron. Al Bielek is the regressed essence of Ed Cameron.

1927: Birth date of Al Bielek. Al's first memories are at Christmas, when he was one year old, and his understanding of all the conversation.

1943: 13 August 1943 – Date of the Philadelphia Experiment. When Ed and Duncan Cameron jump off the U.S.S. Eldridge, they both land in the year 2137.

1953: Final year of Ed Cameron's linear experience. Ed knew too much and irritated Dr Edward Teller. A group of three voted Ed off the Atomic Bomb project and ultimately out of existence as Ed Cameron. Ed is regressed to Al Bielek to the year 1927.

1983: Ed and Duncan Cameron find themselves at Montauk in 1983, after spending six weeks in 2137. Dr John Von Neumann greets the two and convinces them to time travel back to the U.S.S. Eldridge in 1943, to destroy the control equipment and shut the experiment down.

1970 – 1988: Al is recruited to work at Montauk. He keeps the guise of his regular job as an electronics contractor, but works in an altered state at Montauk. He was a program manager for the Montauk Boys program, participated in the mind control experiments, and actively participated in time travel projects.

1988: His memories returned and he believes he was not used any further at Montauk.

2000-2005: Currently, Al Bielek speaks publicly about his involvement at Montauk and the Philadelphia Experiment. Al has been on over 50 radio talk shows and a featured presenter at over 40 conferences.

2137: After Ed and Duncan jumped off the U.S.S. Eldridge in 1943, they landed in the year 2137. They both spent six weeks in a hospital bed recovering from radiation burns suffered from being in hyperspace. Toward the end of their stay in hospital, Ed is moved, by means unknown to him, to the year 2749.

2751: After two years, Ed goes back to the year 2137

Courtesy of www.philadelphia-experiment.com

Since this section is dedicated to establishing a framework for contact, then it might be beneficial to "frame" the following interviews around several suggested protocols. These are hypothetical but I suggest we begin somewhere while we support the discipline of Exopolitics. One such visionary journalist, R. Lee in July 14, 2006 when defining Exo-politics in an article called *UFOs: Exo-Politics: on the D-List said* *"Exopolitics is a non-academic discipline that deals with the implications of possible contact between humans and extraterrestrial civilizations. In a broader context exopolitics deals with the political implications of purported extraterrestrial-related phenomena. Critical questions include what, if any, political framework might be established between human beings and extraterrestrials.* (Wikipedia: The Free Encyclopedia: Exopolitics is on the D-List for some UFO researchers; the poseurs to UFO research and genuine UFO researchers alike may ask the question "why"? What is the issue they have with Exopolitics? It's bizarre to think we can research and investigate -- move towards the Big UFO Answer -- while at the same time utterly ignoring the idea of actually meeting with extraterrestrials.

Protocol One

The Need to Study Exopolitics

The need to develop the disciplined area of study for Exopolitics the way we did for Exo-biology.

- An International panel of inquiry needs to be established.

- Exopolitics should be taught as an academic discipline in colleges and universities as part of the social sciences curriculum.

The Discipline of Exopolitics

Steven Bassett, Dr.Michael Salla, Alfred Webre, the Honorable Paul Hellyer

"Relationship with the Inhabitants of Celestrial Bodies"
MJ-12 draft document Professor Albert Einstein (Princeton University) and Dr.Robert J. Oppenheimer (Director of Advanced Studies Princeton New Jersey)
http://www.majesticdocuments.com/documents/pre1948.php

As part of the compiled Majestic 12 documents leaked to Tim Cooper and studied by the father/son team of Ryan and Bob Wood, this important document completely supports our case for developing "exo-political protocols and developing a public, as well as political policy for contact. No one more than Albert Einstein and Robert Oppenheimer were privy to the *Truth* about extraterrestrial visitation. No one more than Einstein and Oppenheimer could foresee a governmental cover-up and no one more than they would be more fascinated with the idea of alien visitation. This document draft of June 1947 was ironically to reflect what was to happen one month later in July 1947 in Roswell, New Mexico. It is worth studying the entire draft which can be seen on Ryan Wood's website because it is powerful and suggests that these men felt the burden of responsibility to establish protocols for possible "future contact" and thus wrote up their own political document, their own proposal.

In a document draft officially entitled " *Relationship with the Inhabitants of Celestrial Bodies,*" Albert Einstein and Robert Oppenheimer suggest a new international law should be established called the" *law among Planetary Peoples. If these people had their own cultures and laws then we humans would need to accept many of their principles. But also if they reject peaceful cooperation and become an imminent threat to earth, then we would have a right to legitimately defend ourselves. We come to the problem of determining what to do if the inhabitants of celestrial bodies or extraterrestrial biological entities (EBE) desire to settle here.*"

It is curious here that they use the (EBE) abbreviation for extraterrestrial Biological Entities. So I asked researcher Ryan Wood why this term EBE was used in this draft from June 1947 since I believed this term was first coined for the entities in the Roswell crash which happened later in July. He reminded me that the Cape Girardeau crash in 1941 already had these beings aboard and probably the government knew about them. Ironically the suggestion was made by Robert Oppenheimer to submit this draft to the President in June 1947 but rebutted by a handwritten memo (seen in the draft) written by Dr. Vannevar Bush who was against it. There were many people then who suggested that we establish protocols for either accepting these "alien cultures" or for hiding this reality as early as this. Einstein-Oppenheimer also suggest:

If it were a " moral entity? The most feasible solution it seems would be this one. Submitt an agreement for the peaceful absorption of a celestial race(s)in such a manner that our culture will remain intact with the guarantees that their presence not be revealed"

Is this then what started this cover-up, one asks? Here is how Steven Bassett of PRG sees this scenario. "The Paradigm Clock, created and published by PRG in 1998 to track the proximity to a formal announcement by the United States Government confirming an extraterrestrial presence engaging the human race, has been reset to 11:59:45 – 15 seconds to midnight. Such an announcement is formally referred to as *Disclosure* and would mark the end of a 59 year old truth embargo imposed by federal authorities. Midnight on the Paradigm Clock is *Disclosure*. Due to extraordinary circumstances primarily pertaining but not limited to the United States, a window of opportunity has opened for a *Disclosure* event to take place. This window should last through the November election and may remain open or possibly close depending upon the outcome of the election." Bassett further added, "I believe this to be the best opportunity to get past this very difficult transition in human history since the truth embargo was initially imposed in 1947. "The previous setting for the Paradigm Clock was 11:58:45 on March 8, 2004." www.paradigmclock.com/chronicleexplanations.html

This reflects the urgency with which on April 4th 2006, Steven Bassett, who is dedicated to *Full Disclosure* and who is creator of the X-Conference in Washington DC posted this message. Ironically this urgency is also reflected in the other sections of the Einstein-Oppenheimer document which has other concerns. The document suggests that the concept of *res nullius which* means nobody's residence and they state clearly "the moon belongs to no one". So this addresses indirectly the Bush intention to place a base on the Moon by stating that the moon is not property. Einstein/Oppenheimer go on to ask

"the final question of whether the presence of Celestial Astroplanes in our atmosphere is a direct result of our testing of atomic weapons". The

presence of Unidentified space craft flying in our atmosphere (and possibly maintaining orbits around our planet is now however accepted(is defacto)by our military...The use of the atomic bomb combined with space vehicles poses a threat on a scale that makes it absolutely necessary to come to an agreement in this area." They suggest that these nuclear tests have subjected Earth to *celestial scrutiny* and they add *"rightfully so"* and they add that ETS *"could be curious and alarmed by such activity"*. This is an understatement!

Exopolitics as a discipline addresses this issue and its implications and it deals with banning weapons in space. It is common to all of us, Dr. Salla, Steven Basset, Alfred Webre and myself. However, no one is more active in this arena of Exopolitics than Alfred Lambremont Webre, JD, Med International Director, Institute for Cooperation in Space (ICIS)Vancouver, B.C., Canada who writes "humanity's efforts to establish a peaceful world order and comprehensive legal jurisdiction in outer space have been largely shaped by the Twentieth Century world view of the organization of intelligent life in the Universe.. Our permanent war economy on Earth will transform into a peaceful, cooperative, sustainable Space Age society as humanity and our institutions allow a new world view of Earth's role a populated, organized Universe society to predominate in our inner and outer reality, and in our public policies and governmental, legal and political life. The dominant scientific, philosophical, political, social, religious, military and diplomatic paradigm of the Twentieth Century. Its Universal world-view held that all intelligent life ends at the geo-stationery orbit, some 22,242 miles above the surface of the Earth. Likewise, the dominant academic canon of the last century held that intelligent civilizations exist only on our Earth. Alfred Webre has since created the Star Dreams Initiative (SDI) a peaceful alternative to "Star Wars". Among the goals of this initiative is the creating *public interest* diplomacy.

The goals of public interest diplomacy include a negotiated, consensual plan for a mutual, transparent, open interaction and public diplomatic relations between recognized scientific, ethical-religious, and governmental bodies of the terrestrial and specific off-planet culture(s) engaging in a Star Dreams Initiative. This overall plan would include appropriate inter-species treaties under principles of international and universal law. Public interest diplomacy, where appropriate, may include representatives and advisory observers of galactic, interplanetary governing authorities. "A Star Dreams Initiative should develop interactive protocols, setting out the parameters of the project and appropriate proposals for outreach, contact, and public interest diplomacy. These would include interplanetary treaties establishing formal relations and detailing essential functions, such as fundamental declarations of principles governing rights, government ownership, and other key principles of space law, bans on space weapons and warfare in space, outer space exploration standards, security, technology transfer, and interplanetary immigration." These are the key concepts of Alfred Webre's peaceful vision.

Ironically, Einstein and Oppenheimer were far reaching in expressing the same thing when they say,

> *"If the United Nations were a "supra-national organization, it would have competency to deal with all problems related to extra-terrestrial people. Of course although it is merely an International organization, it could have this competence if its member states would be willing to recognize it". (Page 3 Part B)*

They suggest *"a new international law should be established called law among Planetary Peoples and if these people (ETS) had their own cultures and laws then we humans would need to accept many of their principles"* June 1947 draft http://www.majesticdocuments.com/documents/pre1948.php

One interesting attempt to address this issue with the United Nations was made by Sir Eric M. Gairy, Prime Minister and Minister for External Affairs of the Caribbean Island nation of Grenada, spoke before the United Nations, General Assembly, Thirty-Third Session,

32nd Plenary Meeting, on Thursday, 12 October 1978. The key points of Sir Eric's U.N. speech, which is relative to this article, are here.

Article 182: "During our four years of membership in the United Nations we have raised many matters of importance, some of which have been considered innovative, others were current and regular but our views ushered in new thoughts about them, thoughts that aroused new vistas in an attempt to tackle traditional thought-patterns. And still further we have been introducing some very thought-provoking subjects of world importance and world concern, subjects considered by some to be strange and extraneous, but which we feel are sufficiently important and significant to merit our constant articulation and review of them, however and whenever the opportunity permits. Permit me to refer to only a few: the question of women's rights, the universality of God, economic cruelty, the problems of man and his environment, disarmament, man and his material and spiritual behavior, the Bermuda Triangle, unidentified flying objects and extraterrestrial phenomena, decolonization and territorial integrity, human rights, and undue solace given to terrorists."

It is reported that prior to returning home to Grenada Sir Eric visited with President Jimmy Carter, during which they discussed their individual UFO sighting experiences and the pending U.N.resolution. It is also reported that Zbigniew Brzezinski attended this meeting. Sir Eric returned to New York City on March 12, 1979 to meet with the then Secretary General of the United Nations, Kurt Walheim. The official purpose of this meeting was to discuss the fact that on December 18, 1978, the United Nations General Assembly voted to approve decision 33/426, inviting U.N. Member States "to take appropriate steps to coordinate on a national level scientific research and investigation into extraterrestrial life, including unidentified flying objects, and to inform the Secretary-General of the observations, research and evaluation of such activities." The United States was the sole U.N. member nation which unsuccessfully attempted to block that 1978 UN E.T. resolution.

Attempts are still being made to integrate traditional Ufology into a precise political and philosophical framework for humanity. Dr. Michael Salla with his wife Angelika Whitecliff have created *The Exopolitics Institute* to address these concerns and policy issues. I am on the board of directors and am its International advisor because I live in Rome, Italy and travel often throughout Europe. Its mission statement states that *The Exopolitics Institute* is dedicated to studying the key political actors, institutions and processes associated with credible evidence that extraterrestrial civilizations are visiting, monitoring or residing on Earth. The Institute supports the study and dissemination of information and technologies from 'whistleblowers' or 'private citizens' who claim to have physically interacted with extraterrestrials, or had access to covert military-corporate programs involving extraterrestrial technologies. The Institute promotes 'citizen diplomacy initiatives' for peaceful communications and interactions with extraterrestrial civilizations that evidence suggests are interacting with or monitoring humanity. The Institute seeks to prepare humanity for interacting with extraterrestrial civilizations whose existence is supported by credible evidence, and supports full public disclosure by government authorities of all evidence concerning the extraterrestrial presence. The Institute supports the vision of an interconnected global human society that interacts with extraterrestrial civilizations in a peaceful, harmonious and mutually respectful manner."

During the Exopolitics Institute's 2006 Hawaii conference, keynote speaker, former Canadian Minister of Defence, Paul Hellyer echoed our sentiments when he stated in his speech "What are the consequences of the long-time cover-up of extraterrestrial intelligence and advanced technology?

It appears that real government has passed from elected accountable representatives of the people, to an unelected, unaccountable elite

113

group of senior government officials and industrial leaders, an Industrial Military Complex, whose agenda is incompatible with the needs and desires of the population at-large. At least that is my unshakeable conviction. Evidence indicates that the survival of the planet as a reasonably friendly and hospitable environment is at stake, and that vested interests may be blocking plans to save it before it is too late. Even worse, the Military Industrial Complex, that General Dwight Eisenhower warned us about, is creating and producing weapons systems designed to confront visitors from space and, in the process, is proceeding to a situation which could be a sure-fire recipe for a possible conflict. One hesitates to contemplate the unknown and potentially disastrous consequences. Only an early and complete disclosure of the truth can save us from our folly."

We as humanity, even on a grass roots level, must prepare for a possibly staged *Star Wars* scenario. It is unthinkable that we could win such a conflict. The Einstein -Oppenheimer agree when they say:

> "if *Military strategists are planning an attack with missiles with nuclear warheads coming from the sky which will be difficult to determine from whence they came.*" If they are mis-identified, it may cause a space war.

http://www.majesticdocuments.com/documents/pre1948.php

Paul Hellyer, in my interview with him in February 2006, told me he was "deeply concerned because this cover-up involves serious policy issues for Canada and the world. In Hawaii, when addressing the Mj-12 documents, he added "A very recent book, *Majic Eyes Only,* by Ryan S. Wood, is equally compelling. Wood documents 74 UFO crashes from 1897 to the present. While the evidence is much stronger in some of the cases than in others, there is more than enough to convince an unbiased reader that, *first, UFOs have crashed on Earth; second, governments have recovered and exploited these alien technology gifts; and third, most disturbing to a democratic free society, the alien secret is more important than*

Constitutional or individual rights. The war on Iraq involved incredibly bad judgment. Instead of reducing the ranks of the terrorists, it has increased their ranks by 10- to 100-fold. Who are the winners, and who are the losers? The winners are a few large corporations, and those in the military striving for increased budgets. The losers are the people of the world, and especially the people of the United States who are footing most of the bill, both economically and in the realm of world approval. Hope lingers that there may be an end in sight, though certainly it is not for a while, at least. It seems, however, that one blunder leads to another. The US military and their arms suppliers are scrambling to get into a position to take the alien visitors on for size with the technology they have given us. I've received private assurance that the US military wouldn't be stupid enough to do that.

This statement thus takes us to the next subject and next protocol: the identification or misidentification of alien spacecraft and the repercussions for humanity. It is obvious also that our actions over the coming few decades could create risks of major disruption to economic and social activity, later in this century and in the next, on a scale similar to those associated with the great wars and the economic depression of the first half of the 20th century. The United States' position alone, on the ecological question, outraged the entire world during the U.N. climate talks in Nairobi, as it focused on U. S. President George W. Bush who pulled out of the Kyoto Protocol talks. We in the United States have a long way to go and the major players in Exopolitics today are aware that " *someone* is observing this planet and watching us self destruct. The question is "do we still have time?" Is there still hope?

Protocol Two

Our stuff or their stuff?
That is the question.

We need to develop some clarity on our back-engineered alien technology; otherwise we may be shooting at ourselves in our own back-engineered crafts and simulating a space war.

We need some guidelines so we are not misidentifying UFOS.

- Who does the advanced technology benefit?

- What is the military and industrial complex up to and where are the *black budgets* going?

- Will governments chose to disclose the truth or are we doomed to play this "game" forever?

Included in the photo section of this book is a letter by Dwight D. Eisenhower, dated 12th of March 1951 to Eugenio Siragusa. It is obvious that General Eisenhower was aware of this famous Italian contactee who had communication with a human group of aliens who landed at the foot of Mount Aetna in Sicily. The letter says" *Your concern for the future of your children is very natural and understandable.*" The concern refers to the messages given to Eugenio Siragusa, right up until his death in 2006, about the terrible fate of this planet if it continues with nuclear experimentation. Siragusa claims he had over four letters from Eisenhower on personal stationary and if we consider that Eisenhower could have had a meeting with aliens at Holliman Air Force Base during the fifties, this correspondence becomes very significant. What the extraterrestrials told Eugenio Siragusa was this:

30 JULY 1963

"The deadly effects of the nuclear experiments will change everything. The face of your planet will change if responsible men will not sign a treaty. You, terrestrial scientists, cannot vaguely imagine what you have already built and what you still intend to build with your foolish craze of the atomic science. The actual disasters that have killed a considerable number of innocent victims already are nothing in comparison to those that fatally await you in a very next time to come. Complete continents could be shattered from the terrible the enormous force of the cosmic-burning elements. We are still predicting this and nobody, and not even we, could do anything to change the tragic situation in which you are involved. The only thing that you could do to remedy this is to stop each type of experiment immediately that is nuclear. We could only watch, we can not do anything."

This is certainly an exopolitical and ecological concern for our very survival and we were given a warning through the contactees of the fifties like Siragusa and Adamski. We, in the field, are so very grateful for the words and research of Come De Charpentier De Gordon who, although not a UFO researcher, has does an excellent job to seriously address the issues before the world. Mr. Come Carpentier De Gordon, currently the Convener of the Editorial Board of the World Affairs Journal, in his before mentioned Paper: *A Case for Exopolitics: Ushering in a Cosmic Dialogue* presented in Rhodos Greece in 2006, gave us a certain visibility as well as credibility. He does some amazing research to correctly identify the culprits in the cover-up and he mentions the Kennedy attempt to cooperate in Space with the Russians as part of his lecture when he states:

"In 1955, Project Silver Bug was developed at Wright Patterson AFB. It set out to build a "saucer powered by gas-turbine engines". It was only one of the earliest of many endeavors to replicate UFO technologies, many contracted out to leading military-industrial companies (such as Lockheed (now Lockheed Martin), Northrop, McDonnell Douglas, General Dynamics, GE, Westinghouse, Boeing etc...). A seminal contribution was made by the American engineer T. T. Brown who in the early 1950s was able to build a prototype Flying Saucer for the US Air Force and who founded NICAP (National Investigative Committee for Aerial Phenomena) in 1956, one of the major organizations dedicated to UFO research. His lifework is documented in the biography written by P. Schatzkin "Defying Gravity: The Parallel Universe of T. Townsend Brown" (2006).

In November 1963, President JF Kennedy dictated a Memo addressed to the CIA, directing it to cooperate with the USSR to "explain in a credible way the impact of knowns and unknowns" in air and space exploration. He wanted cooperation between NASA and the Soviet Science Academy, a prospect to which many of the "conservative" military and industrial leaders of the USA were bitterly opposed since they regarded UFO-related "black" research projects as essential in the arms race in order to gain superiority in the cold war. There is now a large number of declassified or leaked but verified official reports from various Air Forces, Navies, armies and international military structures such NATO, NORAD et al. about encounters, incidents, chases, dogfights and confrontations with "alien" spacecraft exhibiting properties far superior to any available in the conventional arsenals of earthly powers. For example, there are detailed records about the "Maelstrom missile shutdown" (one among several cases) when in 1967, visiting UFOs deactivated a number of Montana-based ICBM missiles in their underground silos. CNN recorded that President Clinton's former chief of staff John Podesta asked the Pentagon at a news conference in October of 2002 to lift the UFO cover-up.

http://archives.cnn.com/2002/TECH/space/10/22/ufo.records/index.html).

International official policy on the UFO/EBE (Extra-terrestrial Biological Entity) issue appears to have been closely coordinated between the leading military powers, through NATO (reportedly within P.I.40, 54/12) and bilateral contacts between the USA and the USSR to prevent uncontrolled disclosures and leaks. As noted earlier occasional leaks have however been permitted (perhaps because they were not always avoidable) and even encouraged, with "plausible deniability" built in."(De Gordon)

That term *plausible deniability* will appear again below because many whistle-blowers need to use this method to disclose the truth *between the lines*. We see this in the testimony of Ed Rothchild Fouche when he speaks of the advanced triangular craft the TR3B and the new Aurora anti-gravity craft; the craft that he says is created in Area 51 and could easily be mistaken for alien vehicles. In his novel written with Brad Steiger as Science Fiction called *Alien Rapture*, he tells much truth *between the lines*, but leaves an escape with his denial or *plausible deniability*.

His interview in my first book *Connecting the Dots: Making Sense of the UFO Phenomena*, gives the reader details of his subcontracting work at Area 51 S-4 on back-engineered vehicles and the dangers involved with disclosing this fact. This was repeated to me by the testimony of KSC "ground crew astronaut," Clark McClelland, who had knowledge of "Fastwalkers and "Onion drive "and saw those two back-engineered UFOs in Belize while he was on vacation there. Do we already have "warp drive"? Physicist Jack Sarfatti seems to think so when he talks to his fellow scientists who are trying to develop a zero gravity craft. He is trying to visualize "a force field with its gentle push"is an ideal agent for imparting acceleration to the occupants of a space vehicle undergoing high acceleration. With the pushing directly against each internal cell of the body, none of the structure or internal organs of the body tend to get crushed or even strained. In fact, it is easy to prove that if a uniform field gradient provides the total acceleration to a passenger, the passenger undergoes no stress whatsoever. He wouldn't feel a thing, even that he was accelerating."

This description is ironically what Air Force weather observer Charles Hall witnessed while he was on the Indian Springs Gunnery range and the Tall White alien scout craft took the American Generals for a ride in outer space. He says they felt nothing as they traveled at the same speed as if they were one with the craft.

People are always taken back when I show them the footage of what I believe to be a back-engineered craft near Ponte Di Giulio in the Venteo Region near Venice in Northern Italy. The photographer actually waits for the craft to come out of the forest, then it does two 360 degrees turns and then it jets away and vanishes at light speed. That means someone currently must possess this technology because I do not think the aliens made an appointment with the photographer to be filmed over this dry river bed in Northern Italy where the army generally does maneuvers.

I interviewed Jack Sarfatti this year in Rome and although he may not believe totally in back-engineered craft, he has some fascinating ideas in theoretical physics. He is willing to think outside the box and admit to possibilities that are not too popular for conventional scientists. He has stated these possible principles:

1. Einstein's gravity emerges from the coherent phase of the inflation vacuum field.
2. The residual zero point energy density forms both the dark energy and the dark matter at different scales of the pocket universe we are stuck inside of.
3. Since negative zero point pressure creates a universally repulsive anti-gravity field, that is the key to the metric engineering of the advanced extra-terrestrials in their flying saucers

4. Probably Anyon physics is how to phase-lock into the vacuum to achieve the superior flight capability we see in the flying saucers.

5. There may be a theory of how our inner consciousness works and that this principle could be applied to flight because Colonel Philip Corso says that the alien beings (EBE) and craft were one.

It is fascinating that Earth scientists have possibly progressed this far but what is not fascinating is that it is part of the "Deep Black" budget projects that are designed for superiority in war instead of saving the planet from any impending ecological catastrophe. Aliens do not use petroleum-based fuel. Humanity at large could benefit from these technologies.

We are all going towards a new frontier and it is so difficult to break new ground because it seems "insecure". But the implications of Exopolitics leads us to develop not only a philosophy of contact but also some protocols which in this case may need to be set down on the grass roots level. I am sure with all the *formal* alien contacts in the past, there were governmental protocols.

In conclusion as Mr. Charpentier De Gordon so wisely says in *The Dialogue Between Civilizations* will have "to include," sooner or later, those beings and cultures that are not human, in the "homo sapiens" category but which clearly have a presence on our planet and a stake in the future of terrestrial and human life.

Protocol Three

Visitors from the Future and Dimensional Gates

We need to establish if some alien contact simply may be races from the *future* who travel in and out of a "time continuum".

- What if they are connected with "us" from *the future* and have come to warn us of some impending disaster?

- What if they have found the secret to dimensional travel?

- What if we are all related to the "stars peoples" on some level?

- What if we need to rewrite our human history?

It is no secret that the late Colonel Philip Corso thought that the beings from Roswell were a gift from the future. He said that the bodies contained "surveillance microchips "that reported back to the creators and he added that Pentagon was questioning who these creators were? Were they people like us? In his interview in this book, he sadly says that the alien body was the greatest gift, the most amazing discovery because it could travel in space and sustain itself with electro-magnatism. Here Dan Burisch, a Micro-biologist who says that he worked at S-4 on the

Area 51 base gives us a reality that could read as a science fiction tale. Anyone who has personally interviewed Dan "face to face" can see he is sincere in recounting real episodes.

I personally believe any interaction between alien civilizations with direct witness testimony is worth researching! However, my rule of thumb has always been to meet these people "face to face", question them extensively and then watch their expressions. Some people are re-living their experiences and are not making them up. In an article entitled: *Psychology 101: 'Talking face-to-face is best way to spot a habitual liar say psychologists!* –Daily Mail, Sunday, January 14, 2007, his very principle was emphasized. "Research has shown that people are reluctant to lie when speaking to someone else -- perhaps because they feared they would be more easily caught out, either by their body language or tone of voice."

<I found this to be true of Charles Hall and Dan Burisch. Unfortunately, the Dan Burisch case is filled with controversy; much the same controversy that I encountered around the Michael Wolf Kruvante case on which I worked for two years, with a series of seventy audio-tapes and four long extended visits.

The irony is that some main Burisch researchers vouch for Dan because they spent time with him in person and were able to question him but deny that Michael Wolf deserves the same consideration and have been outspoken debunkers of his testimony. We can see the value of real field research here, although it requires money and considerable time.

Both these men worked at Area 51, in particular S-4 facility. Both talk of stargates; both were interfaces for alien guests; both were scientists and both were given permission to reveal their involvement, although some room was left for" plausible deniability" of which I spoke previously. That is how it seems to work. Write a book of science fiction, insert *fact*, as Michael Wolf did, so one can deny your direct involvement and hide the truth "between" the lines.

The Dan Burisch case was first researched by William Hamilton, and then by Linda Mouton Howe, two expert researchers. It was my curiosity and my drive to *Connect the Dots* that led me to Las Vegas twice to interview Dan. It was a pleasure on both occasions as he is a very honest, open and clear in his answers. He just wants to" *Tell the World"* and he does it on his DVD with the same title produced by his friend and Maj-12 sanctioned advisor, Marcia McDowell. She is very important to the story so I asked her for personal information. This is the job description that Marcia McDowell provided to me. She is pretty much a life long friend of Dan and his family, who was formally sworn into Majestic as an operative at the end of 2003 and immediately assigned, per Dan's request, to serve as Dan's operations director. She became responsible for all formal and informal operations, research, communications and publications for Dan and the team. Now, she is permanently dispatched to Dan and the family, to carry on her role in our continuing research. This is customary, in Majestic, for some-body to be assigned to an individual who has held a J-number – Dan sat as J-9 for a short tenure, and so if ever called to testify before the U.S. Congress, he could do so in a capacity as a former member of the Majestic. For that reason she is permanently working in a variety of capacities for Dan and his family.

I thank William Hamilton who wrote the book about this case called *Project Aquarius* for the first opportunity, as we drove from Laughlin to Las Vegas, in 2006 to this scheduled meeting together. Both Dan and Marcia have been honest, cordial and full of information that will stimulate thinking on the part of any researcher.

"The so-called ufology community has been creating as much mess around me as they can, for a few years now. It won't stop and I am not trying to either convince them or court them."

Dan

Interview In Las Vegas with Micro-biologist Dr Dan Burisch

Paola: Dan, tell us, what is your mission? What are your primary concerns?

Dan: Currently I have three main issues on my plate:
1. The Disclosure debriefing going to the public, which has been ordered by the Majestic 12
2. A major biomedical concern, and
3. Continuing my research into Project Lotus.

Other items of ongoing consideration and work are: two books (one underway and one soon to be) and probable music DVDs.

Paola: Every time I hear S-4 mentioned on the secret (not so secret) Area 51 base, I think of Michael Wolf and Bob Lazar who claimed they worked there.

Dan: From the standpoint of Mr. Lazar's description of the S-4 Galileo Bay (4-1), he was accurate but with much less detail than will be presented by us in the up-coming DVD. I have seen and interacted on all four main floors, have seen all four sub-floor access levels and have interacted in three of those four. Should he (Mr. Lazar, or anyone else for that matter) have claimed to have removed any E115 (Element 115) from S-4, that would be an inaccurate statement as NOTHING ever gets out of S-4, except us poor SAP workers...and sometimes not even those!

Paola: Please discuss your work with the creature we call J-Rod. Why was he named that? Was he really a time traveler – and from where?

Dan: Yes, Chi'el'ah (the J-Rod) was from the future...roughly 52,000 years from present. They use time-travel technology to skip and hop in and out of time periods, from a base in the Aquarius Constellation: Gleise 876C. That is the origin of the name for Project Aquarius. That is why they identify themselves as J-Rods, as Gleise 876C is closest to 15 light years from here. The staging base cuts down on time travel acquisition. The J-Rod identified himself to the Sigma Linguistics Team numerically, as he pointed to an "inertial bar" drawing and a J from the alphabet. The name J-Rod is therefore descriptive and sums to 15, as a bar in the Mayan number system equals five and the tenth place in the alphabet is a J. The concept of *Time Travel* is a difficult one. The moral of its (time travel's) story is that every trip furthers a paradox. For instance, Chi'el'ah visited earth in 1973 and, in a subsequent visit, crashed near Kingman, Arizona, in 1953!

Paola: It is important to add that Ryan Wood's new book, *Majic Eyes Only*, talks of the Kingman Arizona crash with some missing aliens. What did J-Rod look like?

Dan: Attached is a drawing I did of the J-Rod a few years ago. We are working on the first DVD as quickly as humanly possible. He had large, expressive eyes and had what seemed like oil oozing from his pores. Attach the likeness I just sent to a crouched, two-legged, large-footed being, with rough, oil-exuding skin, four long toes and four long fingers on each...and you will have a pretty good likeness. He was very ill and it was my job to do tissue extractions, in the Clean Sphere area, with a needle that had a suction device. This was extremely painful for the J-Rod and I seemed to feel his pain also while performing this extraction.

Paola: I heard him called the "Puppet Master" somewhere in my research. Is this true?

Dan: I never personally heard the J-Rod at S4 called the Puppet Master, while I was in charge of the working group. I may have heard something like it in a conversation, early in my work with Majestic, but am not really sure. They usually referred to him as "Stump." I have heard him called "Brightly" and, I believe, "Bright Eyes." I never met the J-Rod at Los Alamos; that would be Bill Uhouse's account. Three J-Rods were in the Kingman Crash: one a present-plus-52,000-years J-Rod, named Chi'el'ah, who was taken to S4 (he's the one I met); one a present-plus-45,000-years J-Rod, who was taken to Los Alamos (presumed to be the one met by Bill Uhouse), and one a present-plus-45,000-years J-Rod, dead at the crash scene. (Bill Uhouse drawing below).

Paola: Were you told not to communicate with him?

Dan: Yes! But that was impossible for they, from the outside, could not control what or how he was transmitting to me. The J-Rod communicated by electromagnetic entrainment; he would "thump" the target (in this case me) with probe signals until he could bring his frequencies into a match with my own. He did it in much the same way as dolphins use their acoustic melons. As he would probe, it would feel like I could fall into his eyes. This is the way the present-plus-45,000 years J-Rods sedate individuals as well, during abductions. They entrain to endorphin response and the auditory center, so while they are relaxing a person bio-chemically, they are telling them (in their own internal sounding voice) to relax. During the time with Chi'el'ah (the J-Rod) he could entrain so that I would feel as though I was actually in the scene and participating in the emotions he was feeling, while he was showing me (for example) where he worked in Gleise. When he would just directly "speak" with me, I could hear my own self-talk (private thought) voice, yet it was clearly of a differing cadence and with different language usage, than my own. He showed me his home planet and talked of his family and the fact that he had a son and missed him. The reason why I pushed was an act of friendship; he had a right to go home, and his mandated stay time had well passed. He asked me to go home. I agreed. He said a couple other things but... well...he wanted to go home to see his son before the crossing is completed. We are not sure how the time re-stacking is going to play out...and he just wanted to see his boy.

Paola: This must be very difficult to understand, especially since it is a time traveler and they could even be "us" from the Future! What does this say about our reality?

Dan: Simply put, as each increase in the paradox occurs, more layers are added into our reality. When we reach the point, after transition, above the plane of our home galaxy, the "cards" are to be re-stacked and the paradox alleviated. The 45,000-years-from-present J-Rods want a catastrophe to be visited upon us as, should it, then our species will be split along logical J-Rods and spiritual (Orions) lines. By the time 52,000 years from [the] present arrives, the 45,000-years-from-present J-Rods will have been subsumed in their society with their ideologies becoming nonexistent. So, to them, a catastrophe will justify their existence. As it stands, should no catastrophe occur (the prevention of which is what we are working toward), the J-Rods may be "re-stacked" (if you will) and possibly wink out of existence, become a non-human-lineage species, or remain as they are with the advent of a new paradox.

Paola: Where is J-Rod now? What happened to him?

Dan: This is where the stargates come in. Some are natural places on this earth and some are artificially created. We created an artificial one in the Egyptian desert, with the knowledge of the Egyptian government. J-Rod was brought there in a stroller and when I heard his plea to return to his family I became instinctive and pushed him through the stargate. I pushed the J-Rod and really didn't see him go in. It just happened as I pushed forward. After that I was "just elsewhere." I haven't a clue where, but I was found.

Paola: Can you elaborate on these stargates and the "Looking-Glass" project? Colonel Corso would describe electromagnetic pillars to me, in the New Mexico Desert, and he said that when they were activated, they would create stargates and things from other time dimensions could come through.

Dan: First, may I start by indicating that I am no mechanical engineer, physicist, or draftsman. The attach image has been composed from memory and is pieced together using existing imagery.

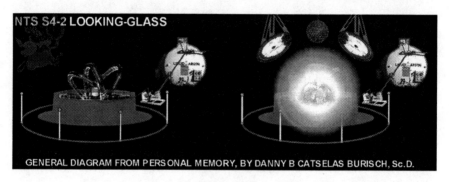

The image on the left depicts what the Looking-Glass appeared like during its slow rotation phase, and on the right during its full operation phase. The objects above the Looking-Glass were cameras, which appeared to be oval disks for intense light collection and recording, and what looked like a geodesic dome above the device, for audio recording. The Looking-Glass was composed from original diagrams for stargate devices, based from ancient cylinder seals.

I should in no way better describe the modified (from the Looking-Glass description) stargate devices themselves, but safe to say they were based on the more general features used in the Looking-Glass. It is true that pillars of the general description, by Corso, are used to "tune in" ERBs, and that tuning is directed toward a stargate device slightly tilted between them. During the present time (2003) return of Chi'el'ah (the present-plus-52,000-years J-Rod) to Reticulum ca. present-plus-52,000-years, I did see three pillars, with golden spheres on top of them, and an apparent geodesic-like cage around the spheres. I should not describe accessory equipment. Two pillars were to the front, with one pillar behind the tilted stargate device. I could only see the third pillar when standing off to one side of the device's area, as the area between the two pillars, in front of the tilted stargate device, was filled with a murky grey oval, which constituted the event area. Both the working Looking-Glass and the activated stargates [had], I noticed, a very pungent ozone odor.

In the Looking-Glass room, once it was activated, it felt and appeared like we were into a round or oval room, even though the room was generally rectangular. It was as though, even though we could see the corners of the room, the space in the room was being bent around the central, activated, bright-pearl-white glowing core. At times it pulsed and I saw a blue shimmer around it.

The activated stargate/portal in Egypt looked dense grey. I was slightly light-headed near it, and even though I could see the oval periphery of the "gate," there was a palpable sensation of a thick "bubble" of electrostatic energy around it. My clothes were clinging with static energy. After encountering it with Chi'el'ah, then finding myself sitting nearby on a slab, I found it very difficult to walk and coordinate. This sensation lasted for days.

When I turned corners in hallways, I would sometimes over-compensate and strike the corner of the hallway. At other times I would under-compensate, making too wide of a turn, then feel dizzy.

Paola: In my interviews with contactees, they say that beings sometimes seem to manifest from a stargate with a shimmering blue light.

Dan: About The Looking Glass technology image: The blue shimmering is around, not inside it. Yes, I believe the blue was created by ozone gas as a byproduct of the interaction between the electricity and the air. If one looks in the center, it is a. cloudy white. Yes, there was some shimmering before the light becomes intense inside the Stargate device, but not when I saw it. It was

already engaged and flat gray; no shimmering. When something comes out of it, it just manifests or is it out of focus, then
it just walks through. I've never seen anything come through,
aside from an early experiment where a person died (at S4),
1994ish.

Paola: What agreements do these aliens have with humanity? I heard
that we split off into two groups after some catastrophe: the J-
Rods and the Orions, who are not that positive.

Dan: What I know as true: There are two sets of treaties, T-9s, which
involve the 45/52 J-Rods, the 52 Orions and us and the OF-
9s, which involve the 52 J-Rods, 52 Orions, and us. Normally,
when I mention a J-Rod, I am thinking of the one with which
I interacted, a present-plus-52,000-years. [Readers Note: these
would be those J-Rods from 52,000 years in our future.] The
present-plus-52,000-years do not usually audibly speak language, but can make 'vestigial' language sounds. The one I was
with had lost the ability altogether. The present-plus-45,000-
years J-Rods can [those J-Rods from 45,000 years in our future]
audibly speak language, to a very limited degree.

Paola: Dan, what do you want to happen with your story? I know you
prefer to work in the field of Microbiology and you just want to
finish this, your mandate to disclose the truth!

Dan: For my personal sake (and my personal peace), before adjournment,
the former MJ-1 ordered that my public discussions of my history
must not extend past approximately September 2007. He ordered
this to protect me – and to make sure I will be available to attend
the 60th. Anniversary party of the establishment of Majestic, to
be held "somewhere" on the East Coast, September 2007! That's
what he told me! But, I will tell everyone straight right now – it
won't go that long! I have absolutely no interest in speaking publicly

(whether by radio or in person) anyway. I have no interest in popularity or playing any PR games! I'll leave that to other people who are interested in such matters. I am fulfilling what I must do, then moving on with my life, research, and publications. I understand that certain things are being programmed in order for me to fulfill my Level 1 orders, and the important spread of this information, so while I am honored by them, I am personally "putting up with" interviews. I find no pleasure in publicity – none. I am, by nature, a researching recluse. That won't change.

Paola: But Marcia is helping by putting out your DVD briefing, which is on my website: **www.paolaharris.com.** It is called *Tell the World* and it appropriately lets the viewer decide because you are telling your own story, instead of having some reporter misinterpret it.

Dan: Yes, that's true. We finally got that done ourselves. Bill Hamilton is among the very best of investigators and has a book on my story called *Project Aquarius,* so that is out. But we are planning:

- a probable book on the emanation of the Solfeggio
- a possible biography
- a highly probable *new Eagles* book
- a continued publication of background debriefing materials via DVDs with anticipated Community Questions DVD
- a highly probable Lotus DVD prior to a possible book on the subject of evolution
- other research publications or books
- tonal relaxation/healing DVDs and CDs

This (God willing I live that long) may go on for years! (I hope I live that long!) None of this, though, indicates in any way my willingness to come out in the public and be exposed to the continual circus. That won't happen.

Paola: I do not blame you. Our own researchers tend to crucify "whistleblower" testimony. I know you have been threatened, so how public do you wish to be?

Dan: You may make this public however you want, if you wish. Bill Ryan and Kerry Cassidy **www.ProjectCamelot.org**, they informed Marcia and myself, last Thursday, that they recently interviewed and filmed John Lear, and that he (according to them) "confirmed" me on video; that he is "convinced" or "knows" that I have been to S-4. I thought that bit of information may be of interest to you. They also interviewed me on film. Bill Ryan and Kerry Cassidy will certainly be sharing with the general public, so we avoid the political issue altogether. They are delightful people. We did the taping in their hotel room. The taping occurred over the 15-16 July, 2006, weekend! My intention is just getting the message out!

Paola: I just posted your DVD on my website because I believe that after all the trouble you had with UFO researchers, you are kind enough to be available. I am aware that the Cyber world lives on gossip and, for us *field researchers,* it is difficult to combat. Give people facts and no one wants to change their minds

Dan: I have just agreed, with Marcia, on a totally separate issue, to give condensed disks away, the bulk amount from about 100 hours of my debriefing, FREE to media and investigators. My intention is I just want the message out.

Danny B Catselas Burisch, Sc.D.
eiecitque Adam et conlocavit ante paradisum voluptatis cherubin et flammeum gladium atque versatilem ad custodiendam viam ligni vitae."
Gen. 3:24

Protocol Four

Viruses and Biological Contamination

We need to protect ourselves from viruses and biological contamination on both sides.

Contact with non-human life forms may cause possible danger to populations and our planet's ecology.

It is an Exo-biological problem that must be dealt with by an International commission.

- Discovery and Disposal Manual SOM1-01. EXTRATERRESTRIAL ENTITIES AND TECHNOLOGY addresses this subject.. Why is it established only for the military?

- Why is this not available to all World Health Organizations? www.majesticdocuments.com

It has always been interesting to me how Exo-biology is accepted as a new discipline in our society especially since it was promoted by the great astronomer Carl Sagan. Recognized in many universities with many graduate and post-graduate courses, it has entered our mainstream academia.

However, it seems that Exopolitics is having a more difficult time in emerging from the "fringe" discipline of Ufology. As I see it, they are both very much connected because we are dealing with strange foreign beings composed of a different biology from the human species, and who may be carrying strange new strains of viruses. Conversely, we are also a danger to them if our biologies do not match and these things should be dealt with before official contact begins. It was not dealt with well in Brazil. The Varginha case for me represents one of the most blatant examples of our ignorance on this planet and our lack of foresight and readiness for eventual contact. This case is one of the most important cases ever researched and AJ Gevaerd's contribution is invaluable to the archive of great UFO crash cases and lacking protocols established to handle them..

The Varginha Case

Briefing about the Varginha Case by AJGevaerd Brazil

Bribe offers

The main witnesses of the case, Luísa Helena Silva and her daughters, Liliane and Valquíria, received the visit of four men who refused to identify themselves. The men were ready to pay any money to make the women deny the story. If the girls had accepted, they would have had interviews in a TV channel out of the city. Another witness was a friend of the girls called Kátia Xavier.

Cover-up maneuvers

Aiming to cover up the evidences presented by the ufologists, the head department of the School of Sergeants of the Armed Forces (ESA), under orientation of General Sérgio Pedro Coelho Lima, launched on May 10th, 1996 an internal investigation to find who among its members were linked to the events revealed about the case.

Military upset

Testimonies about the subject given to ufologists in charge of the case were presented to Colonel René Jairo Fernandes. The officials answered questions on where they were and what they were doing at crucial date and time when the event took place. These were some of the questions left unanswered by General Lima when asked by journalists, who made him upset saying that he did not need to prove anyone anything.

UFO crash confirmed

The first references to the UFO crash date to January 13th, but witnesses revealed that the first capture was made in the morning of January 20th, at 10:30 AM, by members of the Fire Brigade under command of Major Maciel, Sergeant Palhares, Corporal Rubens, and privates Nivaldo and Santos.

Aliens shot with a rifle

Around 2:00 PM on January 20th, members of the Armed Forces made a search at the neighborhood where the creature was found. Witnesses heard sounds of shots and saw the troops carrying bags with something moving inside it. Around 8:00 PM two officers from the Intelligence Service captured another creature which was taken to the Hospital Regional de Minas, and transferred afterwards to Hospital Humanitas, where the creature eventually died.

Pressure and manipulation

The witnesses of the case – which happened nine years ago, already – were put under pressure to remain in silence or to dismiss the events. On the contrary to what many people might have thought, the exposure in the media and the fame the girls got changed their lives.

Threatening calls

Ufologists and main investigators in charge of the case were threatened with mysterious phone calls. The calls were made by unidentified people who had the clear intention to scare the researchers.

Mysterious characters

The housewife Luísa Helena was approached by two men when leaving her job around 2:00 AM on January 18th, 1997. The men were the same who had showed up in her house some days ago offering her money. The men wanted to convince her at any cost to say that everything was nothing but a joke. *"They tried to silence me"*, says Luísa.

Moralist agents

Men in black? Secret agents? Military? Agents from moralist institutions? As institutions and, as moralists we could find many of them. It depends on the sense we can apply to the word "moralist". However, ufologist Ubirajara Rodrigues presents in his book *O Caso Varginha* information which picture that people as belonging to some kind of religious institution.

Operation "Pregnant Dwarfs"

The several contradictions involving the sequence of events presented by ESA commanders show that something strange and abnormal really happened that January morning in Varginha (MG). On May 8th, 1996, General Lima read a press release from the institution stating that *"no element or material from the School had any involvement with the alleged events of January 20th, which dismisses any other testimonies"*.

Some time after that a serious contradiction came to surface. Major Calza, who together with General Lima took part in the release of the official version, appeared in a BBC video saying that *"that day there was a malformed and mentally disabled dwarf who was injured by a hailstorm and, therefore, wandered by Varginha scaring residents together with his wife, another dwarf, who, besides that, was pregnant and ready to breed"*. However, during the sequence of the interview, Major Calza slipped by saying that: *"That was when we [The Army] caught that creature"*.

Injured creature

In the beginning of 2003, the US ufologist and orthopedic surgeon Roger Leir was in Varginha with the objective of gathering information about the case. That time, he talked to another physician who refused to give his name and assisted the captured creature at Hospital Regional. According to the Brazilian doctor, the body had different kinds of injuries, but he was sure that the creature was alive at the moment it entered the hospital.

He stated that when trying to examine the injuries of the being, he suddenly felt *"as if my hands were automatically driven"*, and also believed that *"it was as if the lights in the room had suddenly changed, becoming yellowish"*, it also appeared that *"the perception increased somehow"*. However, he could not understand well the physiological constitution of the body he was examining, although that was something anthropomorphic — with a head, a trunk, and limbs.

The doctor did not hear any sounds which could have been made by the creature, or mentioned the existence of the much commented on *"thin and bifurcate tongue"*, reported by other medical and military witnesses. But he confirmed seen the being's slow movements when showing life signals, and refused to say that the creature seemed to breathe.

AJ Gevaerd Editor Of Brazil's UFO Magazine Interview By Paola Harris

Paola: Now I would like to understand the situation better.......because I thought you said the last creature was captured by a Fireman-.--Was that Chereze? Did he contract a high fever and tumor?

AJ: The first creature was captured in the morning on January 20, 1996 by a team of firemen. The second one was captured by Chereze on 8 p.m. that day. He was a military policeman of the intelligence service of the Military Police, called P2.

Paola: Was there an official doctor's autopsy?

AJ: We do not have any autopsy report, and it was performed by another doctor's team in another town. The man interviewed by Roger was a orthopedic doctor who was on duty as his regular schedule on the night of January 20, 1996 at the Regional Hospital, to where Chereze took the second creature. The medical was asked by the military to take a simple look at the creature and spend only a few minutes with it.

Paola: Why did the creature have surgery if they killed him? Roger Leir in his book said his leg was injured!

AJ: The leg seemed injured BUT NO surgery was made. The alien was almost dead. Nobody killed it, as it was about to die by itself in the few next minutes.

Paola: AJ. This case is so important to the protocols for contact, can you clarify what happened.

AJ: In August 2004, was revealed in Brazil a long interview of researcher Ubirajara Franco Rodrigues with Dr Cesário L. Furtado, one of the physicians who had attempted, without success, to heal the young policeman Marco Eli Chereze, deceased less than a month after having been in contact with one of the mysterious beings captured in Varginha, in January 1996. One of the most serious facts of the "Varginha case" – and one of the most appalling – was the death, on February 15, 1996, of Corporal Marco Eli Chereze, who was then aged 23. As we know, he was part of the secret service of the Military Police (P2) which participated in the capture of the second creature in the night of January 20, 1996. The news of his death spread very fast, during the first months of the investigations, according to other sources, which revealed that a policeman had died because of a generalized infection after having been in contact with the ET. Faced with the gravity of the situation, the subject was treated with extreme caution by the investigators concerned with the case, while the lawyer, and consultant to the *UFO* review – Ubirajara Franco Rodrigues – was still searching for new information.

Paola: Aj. I think that the doctors of the world should have a World Symposium to study this because it happened in Brazil and some-one died. Imagine if it has been children or an entire population. Conversely, Colonel Corso said that the being (EBE) at Roswell faded fast because he was taken out of his electromagnetic environ-ment. We were not even capable of saving them or one of " our own". What else can you tell us about Chereze's reaction? He seemed to keep his composure considering he had a creature on his lap.

AJ: Rodrigues managed to check with the City Hall that a police-man had really died shortly after the capture of the creatures. The ufologist even obtained a copy of the death record, by which he was able to locate the family of the man. The same witness who alerted the investigators about the death of Chereze also declared that the creature, at the moment of the capture, would have attempted a light reaction, obliging the policeman to touch his left arm without his gloves. For some of his colleagues, he would have been contaminated one way or another.

The family of Marco Eli Chereze managed to have an

inquiry opened by the local police precinct in order to establish eventual medical responsibilities for his death. At that time, searches seemed to be doomed to failure, but they are still under way at the present time. The parents did that because, a few days after January 20, a small tumor, similar to a furuncle, appeared under one of the armpits of Chereze. That tumor, according to what was learned at the time, would have been rapidly extracted by the doctor in charge, at the very premises where he was serving. We know today that nothing like happened. But what most drew the attention of the man's family was the lack of information about his health condition and, later, about his tragic death. Even months after his burial, nobody knew exactly the cause of his death.

Paola: If the autopsy were available to the World Health organizations then we could do something about this and establish certain protocols and more importantly inform our populous the way the military does in the *Majestic-12 Special Operations(Som1-01) manual called EXTRATERRESTRIAL ENTITIES AND TECHNOLOGY: Discovery and Disposal?* www.majesticdocuments.com

Why is this such privileged information? What do you know about the Autopsy AJ?

AJ: The police superintendent himself, who lead the inquiry, was not able to be present at the autopsy of the policeman, in spite of his insistence in the face of the police corps in which Chereze served. The retention and/or dissimulation of information regarding that subject were purely and simply an affront to the family of Chereze and to the laws of the Nation. Even worse, such an affront was committed by the Military Police itself. It was only one year after the event of Varginha, on January 20, 1997 that things began to move, after the dissimulation of the facts had been denounced publicly with insistence, both by ufologists and all the press.

Among the most disquieting facts put forward by the investigators, there was precisely the absence of information regarding the death of Chereze, the most important piece of the headache named the *Varginha Case*. Thus, in the middle of a press meeting at the first anniversary of the event, investigators denounced the silence and obtained that the family, the police superintendent and the press had at last access to the autopsy file. From its contents, soldier Chereze would have died from a generalized infection. The policeman would have arrived at home, a certain night after the capture of the creature, suffering from a strong pain in the back. After the ablation of the tumor, he would have shown a gradual process of paralysis and fever which, becoming more serious, obliged him to go to the hospital Bom Pastor where he remained confined and practically isolated from his family during several days. Close relatives of the policeman, especially his sister, Marta Antônia Tavares, the one who went the most frequently to the hospital, could not have contact with him and had great difficulty to meet the doctor responsible for the treatment; and it was even more difficult for them to discover what the illness was. Little time after his entry at the hospital Bom Pastor, the policeman was transfered to the hospital Regional Do Sul de Minas, also located in Varginha, the same where he would have brought, in the night of January 20, the creature he had captured. Chereze was led directly to the center for intensive care of the establishment and taken in charge by the very physician who reveals today publicly what he knows. This is where Chereze passed away at exactly 11 am on February 15, 26 days after his contact with the extraterrestrial.

I am including this in this report with the generous cooperation of AJ Gevaerd Brazil UFO magazine and veteran French researcher Gildas Bourdais both good friends. Gildas and Aj are pictured in the Photo Section. Gildas is in the photo with Dr. John Mack.(note from

G. Bourdais: the following interview of the doctor gives a slightly different story)

"Although all the tests and exams possible were applied in the search of a diagnosis, he could not be saved in time", was to declare the superintendent in charge of the inquiry, in the course of his deposition before the judge of the "COMARCA". It was just discovered that the physicians who took care of Chereze at the time did not have the faintest idea of how to fight the illness which was striking him down. After the decease of the boy had been unveiled before the press present at the meeting of January 1997, the commander of the Military Police of the state of Minas Merais denied the facts immediately, including the presence of Chereze during that night of January 20. But, in order to protect such an absurd story, they invented an even more crude one.

The family of Marco Eli Chereze confirmed that he was indeed on duty that night. Furthermore, he did not die solely because of his professional activities after the contact with an alien, but the creature he had captured died also after that contact, and much faster than Chereze. "It seems clear that the death of the policeman has become the less controllable and the most dangerous piece of the process of dissimulation imposed by the military of ESA and the Brazilian Army", has acknowledged Marco Petit, co-editor of the magazine *UFO*, who participated actively in the inquiry.

A.J. Gevaerd then presents the interview of Dr Cesário Lincoln Furtado by Ubirajara Franco Rodrigues, stressing the considerable research of Ubirajara on Varginha, and the "extreme importance" of this document. Here is now the interview.

What was the cause of the death of policeman Marco Eli Chereze?

Interview of Dr Cesário Lincoln Furtado by Ubirajara Franco Rodrigues (summary by Gildas Bourdais)

Dr Cesário Lincoln Furtado

Researcher Ubirajara Franco Rodrigues (*Ubirajara hereafter*) asks Dr Cesário Lincoln Furtado (*Dr Furtado hereafter*) what was his role in the treatment of policeman Chereze in the hospitals of Varginha in 1996. The following is the summary of his answers to several questions, condensed in chronological order:

Ubirajara — Do you see other interesting aspects to mention about that episode?

Dr. Furtado — Listen, there is that story reported by the family (regarding the capture of the being), about which I don't know anything. But, we don't find any rational explanation for the death of this boy. Because it was terribly fast, you understand?

Ubirajara — Could it be caused by a totally unknown bacteria, however improbable?

Dr. Furtado — Yes. Well, if we talk of something completely unknown, it is obvious that we could not risk any conjectures. There is no answer possible. Now, could something have penetrated inside his organism, something equally unknown, which would have deprived him of his immunity system? This is another question without answer.

Ubirajara — Could you tell what type of thing would be susceptible to provoke that, for instance?

Dr. Furtado — I don't know. That might be an inject able "poison", an infection of injured skin, at the face or foot. It might be an injury caused by a nail, which would provoke tetanos, etc. But we know tetanos. A multitude of things, I might say, and this is just to enumerate some examples of what might have contaminated that boy and deprived him of immune resistance. I repeat that I say that it 'COULD BE".

Ubirajara — Are you telling me that the death of Marco Eli Chereze was a strange death?

Dr. Furtado — A strange death, without rational explanation. In the course of my professional life, I have seen already two persons, aged about 25, die of an infection, but we knew that both had immune deficiency. Both of them, if I recall well, had had removal of the spleen (splenectomy) following a past accident. After a certain delay, that causes immunodeficiency. In that situation, the person may decease rapidly if he finds himself in the condition of a septicemia. But, once again, it was not the case.

This is a classic case of the need for establishing protocols for contact across borders and on a planetary level but also for my true belief that the International community should come together to study this. It is to the credit of AJ Gevaerd in Brazil and Gildas Bourdais in France to lead the way for this futuristic intelligent approach to the study of Cosmic Cultures. They should become part of a team of consultants who are already experienced in dealing with the bizarre nature of these cases. On an exopolitical level as well as the "exobiological" level, we need to do this now. It will save lives. It will prepare us and possibly "them " for a possible "favorable" contact that does not have to end in tragedy.

In general, "The Exopolitics Initiative advocates a decade of contact through public diplomacy with the Extra-terrestrial intelligent beings who are active on and around the earth since several decades at least and who seem to harbor no hostile or predatory designs. On the contrary, some of them at least exhibit real concern for our survival as a species and for the ecological health of the planet. Lt. Colonel Wendelle Stevens (USAF, Rtd.) is one expert who has analyzed data collected over sixty years leading him to the conclusion that the Extraterrestrials who visit us have peaceful intentions. Other prominent scientific names associated with UFO research, with a significant degree of credibility are Robert Oppenheimer, Edward Teller, Hermann Oberth and John von Neumann. In the USSR the eminent rocket scientists Felix Zigel was reportedly involved in this high level scientific quest."(quote by Come Charpentier De Gordon)

Let's suppose the world wakes up tomorrow to find that ETs are here. There is no longer any doubt at all, no room for debate. They're here. Now what? This is the scenario that happened to Charles Hall, a trained Air Force Weather observer in 1965. For me, the Charles Hall case that I investigated held a lot of questions since I knew he interacted with *Tall White* aliens and their children in 1965 in Area 51. I asked," did you shake hands with them? Did you touch them?" Charles answered " Oh no, they might kill you and interpret a sharp move as aggression but he added that the Ambassador or elder Tall White did shake hands with the "Bird Colonel". We, as people, need to know how to act and various investigators on "contact cases" can do much to acquaint us on the expectations of several alien groups. I see this as a chance to share expertise and draw on our respective experiences. As an administrator in Education and a teacher for 30 years, I have a need to write and share information and a desire to learn more. Formal education is the key to future knowledge and with Dr. Michael Salla is designing a full curriculum for a certificate in Exopolitics. This is one solution to the preparation for galactic diplomacy and its challenges. This academic preparation could be considered political science or even social studies and a *visionary* curriculum needs to be developed in this protocol.

Protocol Five

Communication with Alien Races

We need to deal with our fear of *diversity* on all levels.

We can encourage contact with non-human life forms by learning about them first.

- What commonality do we have?

- How many races are visiting this planet?

- Is ESP and telepathy the only way to communicate?

- Do we need to become better" listeners and observers", thereby creating better communication devices?

- How do we foster an attitude of *mutual respect*?

I met Charles and Marie Therese Hall in Roswell New Mexico, at the UFO Museum, in 2003 and I heard Charles speaking about his experience. I realized that he was " recalling" not making up this story. No one until that point had investigated this bizarre case of alien guests with their children on the Indian Springs gunnery range on Nellis AFB in 1965. The more I heard, the more I began to question my own sanity so I called in commercial airlines pilot Captain David Coote and we became an instant *Scully and Mulder* team for a year and a half. In the end, we flew Charles Hall to Indian Springs, Nevada to film his testimony on the spot where he recounts his many experiences. We also enlisted the help of a retired LAPD policeman to help find the other enlisted men with whom Charles Hall spent his time on the base since we had their real names. Forty years had passed but we were able to locate them and still with the kind intervention of this LAPD officer. For the first time in our research, we were able to enlist the aid of a forensic artist from Anaheim California Police department, who on her time off, drew a composite of *The Teacher*, the chief protagonist the Hall story. This case changed my perspective on the level of interaction our government and/ or military has had with these star people for some time. It is an amazing account and it is also one of the very most successful contacts ever constructed by humans with aliens, but then Charles Hall developed his own protocols from his own experience since "no one prepared him for this"!

First Interview with Charles Hall
Colorado Springs 2003

Paola: What evidence that there are Extraterrestrials interacting with Humans on this planet?

Charles Hall: In addition to my own personal experiences, the best evidence that I have consists of the verbal reports given to me during the 1965 to 1968 time frame by the other men who served with me in the USAF. I, myself, do not have any physical evidence, photographs, logbooks, anything printed or written reports. However, over the years, I have seen several pictures and highly reliable reports published in books by other authors that showed and reported on the *Tall whites*. The pictures also showed one of the tall white's scout craft. One of the most interesting reports was published by Alan J. Hynek of project *Blue Book* fame.. He reported having chemically analyzed material that was reported to have fallen out from the bottom of a UFO. In his report, published back in the late 1960's, (not sure of the exact date of publication) he stated that its chemical composition was similar to the composition of slag taken from an aluminum furnace that had been heated to approximately 1100 degrees F (I am doing this from memory and believe that I have the proper temperature). He failed to notice that the chemical composition of that "aluminum slag" is the same as the composition of modern fiber optics that has been heated to its melting temperature. Optical fibers have a chemical composition that is very high in aluminum. If he had noticed the similarity, he would have had strong evidence for the existence of UFOs that also pointed the way towards understanding the construction of their anti-gravity drive power plant. If American scientists would inspect the sub atomic particles that are easily created, (such as meson, baryons, etc) to see which ones can have their path of flight controlled by optical fibers, his work would have resulted in one of the major discoveries in physics of all time. The physical construction of the tall white scout craft and the tall white deep space craft is further described in my books. In addition, in the appendix of *Millennial Hospitality* III The Road Home, I describe my theory of physics entitled "**Hall Photon Theory**". I believe that it explains why the construction of the tall white craft allows those craft to rapidly accelerate to velocities greatly in excess of the speed of light.

Paola Harris: When was your first encounter with these tall white beings?

Charles Hall: In late May of 1965 and early June of 1965. However, it took me many months to control the shock, the terror, my natural fear of them, and to accept the reality of my experiences. As described in my books and writings, for many months I lived in denial of my experiences, preferring instead to believe almost any other explanation for what was happening.

Paola Harris: Were they ever in the company of other military and when?

Charles Hall: Yes. As reported in my books and writings, I frequently saw the tall white extraterrestrials accompanied by UASF Generals and other high-ranking USAF officers.

Paola: Can you speak from personal experience?

Charles Hall: Yes. My three book series entitled *"Millennial Hospitality"*, and associated writings, describe in detail my personal experiences at Indian Springs, Nevada, and my personal interactions with the tall white extraterrestrials, whose Base is located in the mountains north of Indian Springs, Nevada.

Paola: What was your job and position on the Nellis Base? Please state the dates.

Charles Hall: I enlisted in the USAF in July 1964. After completing basic training at Lackland AFB in San Antonio, Texas, I was trained as a USAF weather observer at USAF Weather Training School at Chanute AFB, Illinois. My duties were that of a USAF weather observer during my entire service in the USAF.

In late March or early April of 1965, I was assigned to the weather squadron stationed at Nellis AFB at Las Vegas, Nevada. I was stationed at Nellis AFB from the early spring of 1965 until May 1967.

While I was permanently stationed at Nellis AFB, Nevada,

I was assigned to several temporary tours of duty as the duty weather observer to the Nellis gunnery ranges that are located at Indian Springs, Nevada. Temporary Duty meant that I received extra pay and benefits while serving on the Indian Springs ranges. However, my chain of command, my pay records, and my mailing address remained at Nellis AFB. In between my temporary tours of duty at Indian Springs, I could return to Nellis AFB for duty for various short periods of time. For example, I returned to duty at Nellis AFB for the Christmas holidays of 1965.

As described in my first book, *Millennial Hospitality*, at first, the other USAF weather observers and I shared and rotated the duty at Indian Springs. However, during the late summer of 1965, and at least twice again in the very early spring of 1966, in separate incidents, my replacement weather observers reported being terrified and threatened while out on the ranges. One was very badly attacked and given a medical discharge. Another two-man team of weather observers refused to go out onto the ranges because they reported that they were followed and harassed when they were out there.

After those events, as described in my first book, a committee of high ranking USAF officers and government officials was formed and they decided to send me alone as the primary duty weather observer for the Indian Springs gunnery ranges, while still maintaining the temporary duty status with its extra pay and privileges. I was given special orders, as described in my first book. From that time on, I was stationed almost continuously at Indian Springs. I returned to duty at Nellis AFB only for a few short periods of time to rest and take leave, etc.

F.-DD-214 On 07 May 1967, I was transferred from Nellis AFB to Binh Thuy AFB, Republic of South Vietnam. I was stationed at Binh Thuy from 07 May 1967 until 08 May 1968.

I was stationed at Binh Thuy over the Communist Great Tet Offensive.

Having completed my Vietnam tour of duty, I returned to the U.S. and I was honorably discharged from the USAF on 08 May 1968 at Travis AFB, California.

Paola Harris: Were there others besides you that saw the Tall Whites?

Charles Hall: Yes, the tall white extraterrestrials were seen out on the Indian Springs Ranges by many other USAF personnel. These USAF personnel frequently encountered them at close range in and around the buildings located out on the various ranges during both day and night time operations. Encountering the Tall White extraterrestrials at close range was such a shock that they were frequently reported as ghosts, angels, or as fantastic creatures. For example, weather observers who saw a group of them standing side by side would commonly report having seen a radioactive floating horse named "Range Four Harry." Other USAF personnel would report seeing short glimpses of the tall whites at close range, and then report having had a "Missing Time" experience or having had an unusual dream where he had had daylight sightings of 'dirigibles.'. ..these things were never talked about officially. We would only mention occurrences 'one on one.' .

The only thing that was ever officially said was that the First Sergeant told me that under no conditions was I to ever put a UFO report on the comments or remarks section of. an official Air Force report.

Paola Harris: Do you still think they are still there?

Charles Hall: Yes. I believe that they are still there because the main hanger and their living quarters were permanent constructions located in the mountains at the north end of the Indian Springs valley. The aliens live underground. The main hanger is underground and dug into a mountainside. It has an ideal location. It allows the tall white deep space craft to easily arrive here on earth, land in front of the hanger entrance, and to enter and later leave the hanger without being easily observed and without interfering with civilian airline operations in the Las Vegas area.

Paola Harris: Do you believe that there could be other races on Earth and Where?

Charles Hall: Yes. In the third book entitled "Millennial Hospitality III, The Road Home" I describe the second race of aliens that I have personally met that are here on earth. In my book I refer to them as The Norwegians. I believe that they are coming here from one of the nearby stars such as, perhaps, Bernard's star, which is approximately 5.5 light years away. They might also be coming from the next star past Barnard's star, which is approximately 6 light years away and located in the same general direction. I encountered them in Cambridge Wisconsin in 1961, and again in Madison Wisconsin in the fall of 1962 and in the very early spring of 1963. They look exactly like people from southern Norway, except that they have only 24 teeth and slightly webbed toes. Humans, of course have 32 teeth. The teeth on these aliens have much shorter roots than human teeth, and they can replace any tooth that they may accidentally lose.

This means that they are not limited to only two sets of teeth the way humans are. I would think that there would exist some dentists, both in Madison, Wisconsin, and in northern Europe in other University communities in the colder portions of the world that could verify their existence. Incidentally, as described in my books and writings, the ones that I personally met, had unusually calm and pleasant dispositions. They seemed to want only to fit into our society and enjoy life.

Paola Harris: What message did the teacher give you and how do they wish to interact with us?

Charles Hall: The Tall White female who called herself "The Teacher" explicitly stated to me that all they really wanted was for people to enjoy them, while they were here.

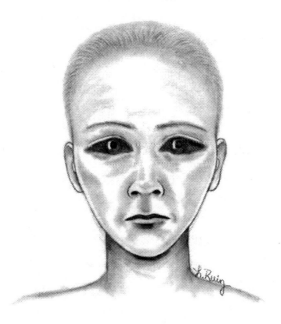

Paola Harris: Why did you write *Millennial Hospitality*?

Charles Hall: I wrote *The Millennial Hospitality* series because I want my children and grandchildren to understand how I felt when I encountered the tall white extraterrestrials out in the Indian Springs valley in Nevada..

"Attempts were made by David Coote to find corroborating testimony from any witnesses to Charles Hall's story. These attempts were met with some success after he was able to track down three individuals who were stationed with Charles at Indian Springs Auxiliary Field during the same period in the sixties. In keeping with Charles' original desire to keep these individual's identities protected (as he did in his books) we shall refer to them as witness 'A' from Michigan, witness 'B' from Pennsylvania, and witness 'C' from Ohio.

My partner in the case, Airlines Captain David Coote says their testimony, though not revelatory, is yet significant in cementing Hall's story in several ways. He states all three witnesses were also utilized as weather observers as Charles had been. They remembered Charles, and confirmed his presence and job as Charles had described. They also recalled everyday, mundane events, and described the place just as Charlie had written in his books. They also remembered some of the other names that Charlie had bantered about.

<u>Witness 'A'</u> Wx observer for Det. 31/ 25th Wx Sqdn (USAF MAC unit). ..also an ex civilian policeman.

Regarding Charles Hall:

"I knew him very well" "Really nice guy – real sweet – hard not to like Charlie." "He was one of those really smart guys...chemistry major or something." "I taught him how to play chess and he knocked me off the Base tournament one time...very intelligent."

Regarding significant events mentioned in Hall's books:

"They [other base personnel] used to come up with this story of 'Range Four Harry'...he was some kind of wild, radioactive horse..." also. .."Charlie remembered that? [regarding an incident where witness 'A' broke a tie-rod in a truck out on the ranges]. ..well I'll be damned... yeah I did that."

<u>Witness 'B'</u> 62 y.o. with a degree in electronics.

"Charlie was a particularly bright character...more studious...more reserved... Didn't talk much about it...we heard rumors constantly [about what went on out on the ranges]...'Range Four Harry' etc. .

Charlie was so serious about it. But he didn't really want to talk about it...I felt he didn't know who he could trust.. ..there were rumors about people getting transferred...if you say too much about this stuff then you might find yourself where you didn't want to be. . ..Charlie spent more time out there [on the ranges] than the rest of us.. ..I believe in him...that he was dealing with something out there. ... I never felt I was alone when I was out there. ... It was a very secure area.

"At one stage he [witness 'B'] had been told from another individual that the Air Police never responded to calls out on the ranges because "...they were afraid."

He stated that witness 'C' "...is a very sincere person."

Witness 'C' "Pushing sixty" Combat veteran. Retired. I'm guessing he wasn't on the ranges for too long.

"Yes I knew Charlie...I relieved Charlie when he left Indian Springs... It was an eerie place...Only knew Charlie a week...he wanted to talk to me about Einstein's theory of relativity...[when witness 'C' first got there, he]...was told to be observant of UFO's. . ..I did feel many times my life was in danger. I'd call the aerodrome officer at Nellis AFB whenever I had suspicious occurrences and they would never confirm any aircraft in the area. . ..a lot of the time I knew I wasn't alone out there; whatever these forces were they were hostile to me because I had a hostile intent towards them." (He admitted he had always been a 'fight first' type of personality).

He felt threatened by certain events that had taken place although he never saw the 'culprits'. There were occasions when "they" would shut the generators off; once, both at the same time...also switched the light switch off in the truck when he had left it running outside in the dark. Witness 'C' stated he had seen unexplained lights out there, both on the ground and in the air. About the time he'd "finally had enough" an incident occurred, when he sensed company and where an "orderly" pile of large 'target posts' (approx 10" by 10" by 15 foot) had been strewn about just outside his range shack one night. He just jumped in his truck and drove back to Base. He told his First Sergeant that he didn't want to go out there again, that: "I've performed my duties to the best of my ability, and I don't care if you put me in the brig." "I recommended that they pull the weather station from the ranges and put it at the radar site on Nellis for security and other reasons...and that's what they did."

"It was either H (witness 'A') or Charlie who...had mentioned to me certain areas not to go...where his ['A' or Charlie's] truck had been 'shut-down'...and other areas where he had had daylight sightings of 'dirigibles.'. ..these things were never talked about officially.

We would only mention occurrences 'one on one.' . ..The only thing that was ever officially said

was that the First Sergeant told me that under no conditions was I to ever put a UFO report on the comments or remarks section of the WAYBAN (sp?) report...an official Air Force document...I'm guessing that apparently there had been a problem in the past."

Says that witness 'B' is a "sharp guy"..."He has been tested as a genius."

So how did Charles communicate with these people? He told me that at first, the Tall Whites had a special helmet with electronics which would shoot a question into his temple if he pointed his head a certain way. With the passage of time, he said they spoke to him in English without using our " contractions" like "don't", instead they would use "do not".

It seems these beings made an effort to adapt to our standards and our language. It needs to be reciprical. Ironically, Albert Einstein in the famous *Oppenheimer-Einstein Draft Document* also brought up this question when he wrote:

> *"relationships with Extraterrestrial men presents no basically new problem from the standpoint of international law; but the possibility of confronting intelligent beings that do not belong to the human race would bring up problems whose solutions are difficult to conceive. In*

principle, there is no difficulty in coming to an understanding with them and establishing all kinds of relationships. The difficulty lies in trying to establish the principles on which these relationships should be based. In the first place it would be necessary to establish communication with them through some language or other..."

http://www.majesticdocuments.com/documents/pre1948.php

When I published and researched the Charles Hall Case, with Pilot Captain David Coote, it opened my mind to the bizarre reality that aliens could be living among us and alien children could be interacting with human children. We are all going towards a new frontier and it is so difficult to break new ground because it seems "insecure" but the implications of Exopolitics lead us to develop not only a philosophy of contact but also some protocols, which, in this case, may need to be set down on the grass-roots level. I am sure that if there were "formal" alien -government contacts in the past, there must have been some preliminary protocols established. The Billy Meier case has some specific ones that we need to consider although these are the most human like aliens recorded.

The Billy Meier Case.

Schmidrudi, Switzerland

In 2005, I went to Switzerland to speak to Billy Meier with three of my Italian friends, also researchers. Although Billy is very protected by his group called FIGU, I was able to walk the grounds, see the fantastic array of vegetation that grows there in that atmosphere and ask plenty of questions. FIGU told us that Billy had several attempts on his life and they were careful to screen visitors.

On Sundays, the mountain chalet complex called the Semjase Silver Star Center is open to the public. At 3:00 AM, they have their Peace meditation in German and since we could not understand the language, we went to a beautiful flowering meditation garden on the property to meditate by ourselves. All at once, I looked up and I saw Billy Meier standing by the fence staring at me. I know he was checking us out. Minutes later he sent Guido Moosbrugger, his Austrian biographer, who had been following the case for twenty years, to us to answer our questions. I understood that Billy treasures his privacy. Moosbrugger wrote the very comprehensive book *And Still They Fly* about the Meier Case which I recommend to everyone. It is an excellent book on this contact case with human like aliens but mostly it discusses what we are discussing here: the protocols for contact.

In one chapter (Pages 104-105), the Pleiadians say that their aural vibration is so high intense that they have an irresistible influence on a human being in search of truth. "If unprotected, the pleiadians are enormously susceptible to the vibrational realm of the average Earth citizen and the unavoidable consequence is hopeless confusion combined with a feeling of anxiety and they act illogically and uncontrollably. Therefore, the Pleiadians shield themselves against the vibrations of Earth people especially if Earth people are less than 90 meters (297 feet) from them. For security and safeguards, mechanisms are used to keep these vibrations away so they will not be injured. (Page 60). We see that the Pleiadian ship possess a protective shield that prevents 100 percent against the negative vibrations, including the relatively low frequency vibrations of Earth people. They also claim to have a mechanism on board that can measure the brain waves of an approaching human being to see if he will become violent or will panic with fear.

Billy says that he possessed the attributes that a contactee must always have at his disposal. Among these requirements are primarily the command of spiritual telepathy and the ability to keep his own thoughts under control, and if possible, not radiate any negative thoughts feelings and vibrations into his environment. We are a" violent" species and so it is logical that some more evolved Cosmic Cultures are taking these precautions. The question is what precautions are we taking? It is time we put something in place. I have often said that we do not handle *diversity* well on this planet so how could we handle it with the advent of Cosmic Cultures?

That brings us to another challenge. What would one do if he ran into *Bigfoot* in the forest? The following interview opened my mind to this reality. Jack Lapserrities (Kewanee) has a great deal of video footage which he is not making public yet. From seeing the film, I realized that this is a *realty*. This video footage taken all over the world proves, beyond a reasonable doubt, that these alien species exist. It impressed me greatly but also it complicated my research because I did not realize that spacecraft and alien greys were also seen with *Bigfoot*. Everything must be considered if we are dealing with communication with alien life forms.

Interview with "Kewanee" Jack Lapserritis. M.S.

Author of *The Psychic Sasquatch and their Et Connection.*

"I don't know who you are but I will not harm you"!

Paola: Jack, when did you first start researching the " *Bigfoot* Phenomena in particular? Were you first interested in UFOS before you became interested in *Bigfoot*?

Kewanee: I prefer to be called by my Native American name Kewaunee. Actually I was always interested in UFOs, and other strange phenomena but strangely enough I started becoming interested in *Bigfoot* fifty years ago when I was 12 years old by writing to different universities, different places and people in different areas. For instance, I would write to Harrison Hot Springs, British Columbia in care of the Postmaster. But in the 50's, at the age of ten, I was interested in UFOS. Why I was interested? I don't know. But there was little information out there. Why? I don't know but at twelve I heard of Bigfoot.

Paola: I heard you say you were in the military for four years and traveled a great deal and you had ten years college and four degrees, mostly in anthropology.

Kewanee: Yes; I was in the United States Army Security and did travel.

Paola: Ok. So how where you raised as a young boy?

Kewanee: I was raised in both western Massachusetts and Vermont. We had a big house in each state. I started by *Bigfoot* research in 1956 in Greenfield, Massachusetts. My father was a hunter and fisherman and there was an article in STAG magazine about the Sasquatch and that is my first experience of something like that existing. That's when I wrote to Rutgers University and several other places but mostly Canada at the time and I addressed it to the Postmaster of every city. I knew the Postmasters were working for the government at the time and they would have to answer me. I would send the article on *Bigfoot* and they would give me their understanding of the phenomena. As I traveled all over the world later on in England, East Africa, Japan, Australia, I continued my curiosity. I did an anthropological study living among the Takuna Indians in Bogotá, Columbia. My mother would send information and magazines when I was out of the country for five years.

Paola: At that time was there only that one picture of *Bigfoot* with a film. Correct?

Kewanee: Yes. the Roger Patterson film was taken October 7th 1967. I was living in Ethiopia at the time and that film had been analyzed over and over again and the scientists who just looked at it at the Smithsonian and they called it a fake. But today even the lay person can see the rippling muscles in all the right places, in the legs, in the shoulder-blades. Other scientists have noticed that. It was brought to Russia and analyzed for six years by physical anthropologists and they analyzed frame by frame like scientists should do. Why the scientists in the United States did nothing is a shame on them. Why don't they do the same thing?

Paola: The same reason they don't do anything about UFOS and the paranormal and ESP. This is not part of the "data bank" of our western culture. It refuses to go there.

Kewanee: It is absurd. Well if you recall last week, the TV program 60 MINUTES in August 2006 said this government scientist quit because the Bush government refused to acknowledge "global warming". They wanted to say that it was not happening. There is overwhelming evidence for this but George Bush and his father have investments in fossil fuel and continue to deny the truth about "global warming". So I think many scientists are threatened and told that you cannot put the "Bigfoot" information out there.

Paola: In my future book on Exopolitics, I am speaking about protocols of future contact with extraterrestrials. "Bigfoot" is a dimensional reality seen all over the planet. Can you give me three suggestions about how people should act if they encounter a Sasquatch in the woods? What should *the Protocols be;* the things they expect humans to do?

Kewanee: The most important thing is to be totally non aggressive. If you have a gun, lay it down. If you have a holster gun, take it out and lay it down. Let him see it. He can see it and he knows what it is. You may say "I may need that to protect myself." But they run 70 miles and hour. They can get a hold of you and they can flip a car with one hand. They are incredibly powerful but you see nowhere where it is attacking people. Be "non aggressive", even in your mind. Back in 1981, I interviewed three people ages 19, 20, and 22. They said, "we don't understand. It was a 7 foot Sasquatch. We ran into an A-frame mountain cabin. It pounded on the doors. It broke the window in back". They said it was going to kill us. I told them "no it wouldn't," They said it attacked them. "No. Pounding is not attacking" I added and asked them what they were thinking at the time. One young man said that, "if I had a gun I would have shot it"! Well, they were projecting their thoughts and it can literally read thoughts.

Paola: Then these beings can read your mind and these people did not realize it because they were not aware of telepathy.

Kewaunee: Right. They were projecting unwittingly all their negative thoughts to them.

Paola: Don't the Sasquatch know we don't use telepathy on this planet.

Kewanee: Of course, but that is to their advantage, isn't it? I would also be thinking warm thoughts towards them. Just think in your mind " I don't know who you are but God bless you. We will not harm you in any way". Just think it. He will know that.

Paola: You said it is "a give and take" between food and gifts. You interact with these beings. They understand giving and taking.

Kewanee: Yes1 I've left crystals for them.

Paola: They disappear? They are not there the next day?

Kewanee: There would be rocks there or sometimes herbs are left for me. I am a master herbalist. They leave certain things where can ask what herb is this, they tell me telepathically what it is for. For years I stayed in a cabin. If I leave food then they leave things back. My cabin is in the wilderness area. There is nobody there.

Paola: You said you saw three different types. Which types have you seen?

Kewanee: I have seen the ape-like type called the Sasquatch and those we call the "Ancient Ones" that have far less hair on their faces. I've seen ETS with them. I've seen small people. I saw one in particular with slanted eyes sharp features and a space suit on. I've seen those from the Pleiades that look like us except that they are tall. The woman about 6'3" and the two men 6'4"and 6'6" inches and they literally projected themselves down in the middle of a friend's living room and stood there. They had full suits on.

In January 1991, four 6 1/12 feet tall Katchina appeared at the foot of my bed in Sedona, Arizona. I was staying in the house of an Indian medicine woman, and as soon as I turned the lights, they appeared. You could hear their feathers rustling. You could hear the bells around their ankles and they talked to me for roughly 50 minutes. They talked to me about my life. They are ETS basically. They are in the Hopi traditions. I understood what unconditional love was and being non- judgmental because of how they spoke to me. It literally changed my life.

Paola: Last question. Do you ever think we will know the truth about the Sasquatch? Will they ever come forward? Did they say more people will see them someday'

Kewanee: They want it out more and more because more and more forest land is being destroyed. My feeling is that if the cleansing of the planet happens around 2012 and several billion people die, and plagues, perhaps earthquakes happen on a massive scale globally, then that is when they will want to help and they will really come out.

Paola: Then you believe in that prophesy about problems in 2012.

Kewanee: I sure do. The Mayan calendar is the most accurate calendar in the world far more accurate than the modern calendar.

Paola: Then they told you that we are in for some tough times ahead.

Kewanee: They told me to put food away, water, warm clothing in several places in case someone discovers it and it happens. They said we will be safe in the woods but they live underground. They go underground

Epilogue;

Jack Lepserities (*Kewaunee*) has written the most interesting, comprehensive book on *The Psychic Sasquatch* covering most sightings in this planet. He has a unique relationship with *Bigfoot* but as a researcher interested in anthropology, he also cites details of actual human interaction by interviewing 139 people in his book. He told me he even spoke with Dr. Allen Hynek who was very fascinated with this aspect of the phenomena.

There are many varieties. The Yeti who are white and seen in the Himalayas, the reddish brown ape-like ones seen everywhere in the United States and those he calls the "Ancient Ones" who are humanoid and have less hair and are very intelligent. Some beings are woman who are nursing their young. Most live underground and also exit from dimensional portholes and are aware of their human neighbors. These natural dimensional potholes have a shimmering effect in the forest and are described by witnesses. It is the same "shimmering dimensional porthole" effect that I asked Dan Burisch about.

Because of the quantum physics principle of "non locality", Kewaunee believes this being can appear anywhere as the ETs do now. Kewanee showed some astounding film footage of one young Sasquatch looking right into the video camera. He also showed many photos of these beings walking upright like us through the woods and taking food from people's gardens. He has also collected hair and feces samples and he has several large casts of its footprints; so this proves that there is a great deal of concrete evidence to study. Even more interesting is this relationship *Bigfoot* has with the Extraterrestrial races. They and we may be genetically engineered races. Today we have many films and photos to add to this evidence. All this needs to be examined scientifically as it is a reality. Since spaceships are the common occurrence around *Bigfoot* sightings, Kewanee encourages us to revise the scientific paradigm of research to include expert witness testimony concerning Bigfoot.

For me this is a perfect example of why it essential that friendly exopolitical protocols are in place for future contact. It will enrich our lives to encourage a friendly relationship with these kind-hearted beings and other visiting races. We need to consider those cases that truly happen that are totally bizarre. Who was the being that appeared in this school in Naples? Did a dimensional " port hole" open up to accommodate his appearance? The following case leaves more questions than answers.

A real case near Napes Italy appeared in the Italian Newspaper *"La Republica"*

28 April 2005: Mysterious humanoid seen In Campania region near Naples

What the researchers are now investigating is a Close Encounter of the Third Kind; witnesses are still under shock. When the press published this news, last year, a team named Ufoitalia (http://www.ufoitalia.net) said they were actively studying this very important case and announced the release of photos, evidences and further details within few weeks. They also claimed that, to protect the privacy of more than thirty witnesses involved, and due to the fact that the sighting took place in a very important school, they would not make public the name of the town or the name of the school. They mentioned only the name of the Italian region where the facts happened: Campania.

(Note of the translator: Sadly, at the moment we must note that, more than one year after the facts, the so-called "Ufoitalia team" has done nothing, has released nothing, and their site reveals a desolating tendency to recycle old news with the only aim of sensationalism. Like too many web-ufologists, they only make a lot of noise, looking totally incapable of operating in the field and, considering that Ufoitalia gave out no names and that Campania is one of the biggest regions in Italia, with hundreds of towns and schools in its territory, they stopped other researchers from studying this case and the result is. Once again, it was the triumph of Cover-Up.

This is the testimony of the first witness who required an investigation from the Ufoitalia team: Let me introduce myself to you. I am the headmaster of a secondary school in Campania. I am an old man and I never believed in paranormal phenomena or in UFOs. But a shocking experience, involving all the 500 students of my school and their professors (everybody got interested in the phenomenon with astonishment but also with fear), made me to reconsider my bias. In fact, on the day 28 of April 2005, more or less at 11.40 a.m., in the corridors of our very respectable school, I saw, together with Professor I.S and Professor S.M, *a creature of indefinite shape,* completely naked, holding in its hands a strange object (it had hands but they were not human; they were something like claws). We panicked and ran away and the creature did the same. Its escape was seen by at least 30 students, who later confirmed they had clearly seen it running. After this, the creature disappeared. I well understand how all this story could sound very strange. Like all the other school professors, I would never believe that such things could happen. Newspapers did not want to spread this news and when we called local authorities they only limited their action to a superficial inspection but, having found no traces or footsteps, simply ignored us, almost laughing at our words, saying it all sounded too absurd to be real. So we encourage you to come to our school to do a serious investigation."

Protocol Six

Record, Collect, and Decipher the Cosmic Messages

It is essential to record, to collect and to decipher the cosmic messages of all types.

- Who is in charge of collecting this data?

- Are radio telescopes antiquated technology?

- What is role of psychologists and psychiatrists in "contact cases"

- Do contactees really carry messages?

- Do any messages convey *Hope*?

This is the message that appeared in the "Crabwood" Crop circle that has an alien face that is carrying a digital disk. It was studied and when deciphered reads:

"Beware the bearers of FALSE gifts and their BROKEN PROMISES. Much PAIN but still time. There is GOOD out there. We Oppose DECEPTION. Conduit CLOSING

To me, this seems like a mixed warning from the stars. It says *to trust no one* and it warns of the closing of the "conduit" or communication. It leaves us a bit sad. But it continues to say, *there is still hope!* On the other hand, *The Aricebo Reply* crop circle in Chilbolton England has an image of a grey indicating that he came from a planet that had silicon-based life system. It includes an altered reply to our messages sent from Aricebo Puerto Rico facility. These images should be studied as specific research that I call " cosmic messages" because we are being given the answers to questions asked and we are ignoring them.

Several new books and cases this year illustrate that we need to decipher symbols. Art Bell interviewed author Jim Sparks (*The Keepers*) who has been abducted by various aliens for the last 18 years. The aliens informed him that the earth is very close to "the point of no return" and that we are killing it off with our pollution. They had said it still is possible to save the earth and that the rainforests are the key. They are the "lungs" of the planet. The aliens are saving seeds, plants, animals and various things from here in case we don't make it or a Noah's Ark, worst case scenario. What is interesting is that the *Phoenix* is becoming a common symbol. In Chapter 14, called My Daughter, "He learned that aliens also use symbolism as we use the flag, to represent leadership, government, or some sort of organized structure. He has come to believe the *Phoenix* symbolizes something very deep. It's universal in nature. It represents the organized structure that is in the process of saving this dying planet from complete environmental destruction. Sparks also believes this symbol represents several different species of aliens from all parts of the galaxy, and perhaps other dimensions. This includes humans, the same humans who have been members of this secret club for a very long time. The *Phoenix* is as symbol all of us should keep an eye out for." http://5thworld.com/Postings/7P6Y5W4W.html

It is ironic that we have so much alien craft phenomena called the *Phoenix lights* in Phoenix. Arizona. I have noticed the murals depicting this mythological bird at Sky Harbor Airport, another symbolic image of a bird rising from the ashes of total destruction. It is interesting that NASA has just adopted this symbol for its future Mars missions. The symbol is for the Phoenix Mars Lander. Does this mean from earthly catastrophe we will reconstruct "human life" on Mars?

What is that a symbol for? It could be the fast accumulation of problems caused by ecological pollution, sociopolitical decay, genome fund depletion, and exhaustion of natural resources. If humankind wishes to survive, a new strategy must be adopted. One such strategy suggested is the " opening of the heart" suggested by Dr. John Mack. What is most memorable is a spiritual intervention which was an enormously effective tool. Many remember the 1988 Harmonic Convergence of Jose Arguelles. It brought the Planet together. There are many people in the field who are working hard in this effort.

Interview with Yvonne Smith (Psychotherapist)

August 2006

The Messages From Contact

Paola: Yvonne, you are the creator of CERO. Can you describe the objective and the membership of CERO? What is your website?

Yvonne: Here is my answer about CERO.

CERO (Close Encounter Resource Organization), a non-profit organization, was founded in 1991, with a small, core group of members, charter members if you will, who were instrumental in helping me establish ground rules and the, now famous, name. The objective of CERO is to provide a "safe haven" for those individuals who have had a UFO encounter. As my hypnotherapy practice grew, I realized that many of these people had no support system; they felt isolated. During the CERO group meetings, members are allowed to share their experiences, cry and laugh with one another, without the threat of being ridiculed. They have become a family to one another.

CERO members, past and present, consist of people from all walks of life: doctors, lawyers, college professors, film industry personnel, construction workers, postal workers and housewives.

After founding CERO and becoming involved with so many individuals who had experienced "close encounters," I quickly learned that there was world-wide interest in this subject. Since then, I have been asked to make 40 to 50 television appearances and radio interviews, both in the United States and in Europe. The same international interest resulted in me being asked to lecture, not only throughout the United States but also in South America and Europe.

My website is: http://ysmith.com. My email is: yvonne@ysmith.com

Paola: Yvonne, you are currently becoming more active since you took a few years off. Tell us what inspired you to return to your life's passion? When did this happen?

Yvonne: Because of some difficulties in my private life, I found it necessary to take a hiatus of a couple of years. My return began to occur in January of 2004. Individually, CERO members were calling, urging me to get the group back together. The magical aspect to this is that the members did not know that the others were calling. It was truly synchronicity. Once this happened, I realized that there are still hundreds of people who are having experiences who need help. CERO members inspired me to return and continue my "life's work."

Paola: How has the UFO field changed over the years?

Yvonne: In the last few years, the research shows that abductions have not slowed down and the aliens are rapidly improving the hybrid program. In past years, the hybrids were very unique looking and could easily be identified. I recently visited with my colleague, Dr David Jacobs, in New York, who reinforced the belief that the goal of the aliens is to integrate these hybrids among us, unnoticed, in our society. Of course, there is a tremendous amount of work yet to be done in this area.

Paola: What do you see as different in your hypnotherapy group?

Yvonne: Over the years, I have seen tremendous growth in CERO. Members have spent years processing what they have experienced and incorporating it into their daily lives. Their spiritual growth is truly inspiring. In recent group meetings, they have discussed the realization that, if they live their lives in a positive way and extend themselves to others in a positive way, the world can be changed. The established members are now helping and assisting new members to deal with their UFO experiences. You have just returned from New York. You said that you saw Bud Hopkins and David Jacobs and you attended a Linda Cortile lecture. So many people are interested in this abduction because it, supposedly, involved the Secretary General of the United Nations. What year was this abduction? Tell us what you learned in New York.

Yvonne: The Linda Cortile case is not only interesting and compelling but, recently, while visiting, my colleague, Budd Hopkins and his Intruders Foundation, in New York, Mrs. Cortile graciously took me on a personal tour of the [sites of the] events of that fateful night. The abduction occurred on 30 November 1989, at approximately 3:00 a.m. in New York City. There were many witnesses to this case, including two New York City police officers and a very influential political figure. During Mrs. Cortile's lecture, she spoke about her personal friendship with the late Cardinal John O'Connor, suggesting that the hierarchy of the Roman Catholic Church is interested in the UFO phenomenon.

Also, during the seminar, two other witnesses, who, at the time of her abduction, were employed at the New York Post, came forward to briefly talk about what they saw that night. As a result of my New York visit, I expect that there will be more developments in the near future.

Paola: You met Colonel Corso in Italy for San Marino [conference] 1998. What did you think of him and his disclosure?

Yvonne: My visit to Italy and San Marino in 1998 was truly a memorable experience, where one of the highlights was meeting Colonel Phil Corso. As I was taking in the sites in Rome with the Colonel and his family, I enjoyed listening to him talk about the war and the time he spent in Rome, back in 1944 and 1945. His book *The Day After Roswell,* is intriguing, as he describes how the 1947 Roswell crash helped develop reverse engineering. He wanted the truth to be known. He told me that the public and the young people had the right to have this information.

I have always appreciated that you, as a close friend of Colonel Corso, gave me the opportunity to meet him and hear some of his experiences.

Paola: You have been made a Producer and Associate of Lisa Davis and The Hollywood Conference (NUFOC). What are your plans for disclosure by way of this Conference?

Yvonne: As producer of the NUFOC (National UFO Conference) and colleague of Executive Director, Lisa Davis, the plans are still underway for the spring of 2008. We expect to emphasize the Contact and Abduction aspect of UFO encounters; a subject that is too frequently not covered at conferences.

Aliens living among us:
Book: Raechel's Eyes

Interview with Helen Littrell
December 2006

Two years ago I became curious about a book called *Raechel's Eyes* written by Helen Littrell and Jean Bilodeaux. I called Helen because it was her blind daughter who accepted the hybrid girl Raechel as a roommate. Jean Bilodeaux, who is a Mufon investigator, did a fine job of getting the details and researching this fascinating case. I met both women in Laughlin Nevada UFO congress some years ago. The story is too incredible and filled with important political implications and policy issues and reflects the *Einstein and Oppenheimer* document concerns about aliens relocating among us and what the consequences would be. It is a haunting story to a researcher like me to know that there are hybrids among us but then I remembered that Clifford Stone, who worked on many crash-retrievals, once told me that entire extra-terrestrial families have been relocated on this planet. I strongly recommend *Raechel's Eyes* to all who want to be acquainted with how we could possibly integrate *Cosmic Cultures* into our society. Talking with Helen recently, I realized she remembers so much more than she wrote and has much more to tell. It is obvious that these people like her who have lived the experience will know the protocols involved and become our *off- planet* cultural consultants of the future. Her interview alone answers many of my protocols for contact questions.

Paola: Do you know for a fact that aliens or alien hybrids are among us? How?

Helen: Aliens and alien hybrids have been present among us on Earth for at least 35 years that I know of. The first personal contact that I am aware of with alien hybrids was when I met Raechel Nadim in the spring of 1972 when she had been placed with my daughter, Marisa, as a roommate in an apartment complex near a junior college where they were both enrolled as freshmen. A few months later I visited a Top Secret military installation called *Four Corners* where I met another hybrid, a geneticist involved in an ongoing exchange program between his home planet, Zeta Reticuli, and the U.S. government. This was the same hybrid who had helped with Raechel's upbringing after her rescue from a downed craft several years previously when she first arrived at Four Corners. I cannot say that I have had personal contact with an alien *per se*, although I have been abducted several times over the years. Although I always know when this is about to take place, there is never any conscious recall of events that took place during the abduction. I do, however, believe that alien beings are responsible for my abductions and I am quite certain that I have some level of interaction with them at those times.

Paola: Was there any military intervention that was involved that you saw or experienced?

Helen: Soon after meeting Raechel face to face at the apartment and realizing immediately that she was not human, her father, Air Force Colonel Nadim, set up a meeting between me, my daughter, and himself to explain her background as well as his. His first duty station was at Four Corners, a Top Secret underground installation that for all intents and purposes did not exist but was an integral part of the Humanization Project.

Raechel's special food and drinking liquid were left outside the apartment door at specified intervals by members of the Humanization Project who also appeared approximately bi-weekly to interview her and discuss her progress. I personally saw three of these so-called "men in black" as they were leaving the apartment. We met on the stairway, and their appearance was extremely menacing and I was frightened. I also saw their vehicle in the parking lot on two different occasions. It was a vintage 1930s shiny black Cadillac that resembled a World War II German Army staff car. Its license plate was also unique.

Paola: How did you know Raechel was not human? Describe her.

Helen: As I left the apartment one evening after visiting my daughter, I met Raechel quite literally face to face. She apparently tripped on something and it was evident she was going to fall straight forward. I reached out and caught her arm to break the fall. In doing so, I found myself holding onto skin that in no way felt human. Her face was inches away from mine. The large, wrap-around sunglasses that she always wore indoors and out slipped down on her nose, revealing her huge eyes that slanted upward out onto her temples. They were avocado green in color with vertical black slits instead of pupils. I was positive that she was not human. A subsequent meeting with her father, Colonel Nadim, provided further acknowledgement that she was indeed a hybrid human/alien. Raechel was about 5'4" in height, slightly built, with long, thin arms and legs. Her skin was a pale orange/greenish color, and her hair was wispy and light reddish-blonde. She was actually fairly attractive once one got past her unusual features.

Paola: Was she able to get along well with humans? What were her major disadvantages?

Helen: Raechel appeared to interact satisfactorily with humans, especially my daughter, Marisa. In fact, they became close friends and there were other classmates who knew her socially. A major disadvantage was her speech that was always somewhat mechanical and conveyed little emotion. Additionally, she had almost no font of knowledge that would be normal in a young female college student. She dressed exclusively in jumpsuits with long sleeves and wore a scarf tied around her head and she wore large wrap-around sunglasses. This outfit was worn indoors and out. However, since she remained somewhat withdrawn and deeply involved in her studies, none of these unique characteristics appeared to be problematic to her.

Paola: What happened to her?

Helen: Raechel disappeared suddenly and with no warning in late spring of 1972. My daughter returned to the apartment for lunch one day and discovered that all of Raechel's possessions were gone. Panicked, she called me at work and I, in turn, contacted a friend in Base Security at the installation where I worked, asking him to check on Colonel Nadim's whereabouts. Minutes later I was notified that he was also missing, as were all files pertaining to him. It was as if the two of them had dropped off the face of the earth.

In 1998 during hypnotic regression, I discovered that members of the Humanization Project had determined Raechel had acquired a greater degree of emotion than was desired, and that because of this they had disposed of her. I learned that they had pushed her down a steep, dark flight of stairs to her death. This was reinforced during an abduction in 2005 where the actual scenario was played out in front of my eyes and I was restrained forcibly from attempting to help her, allowed to be merely an observer.

Paola: What protocols do the citizens Earth and we as Galactic Diplomacy advocates need to adopt for future cases like this? How can we be prepared?

Helen: It is obvious that as citizens of Earth in general and Galactic Diplomacy advocates in particular, we need to publicly acknowledge the huge number of human-alien hybrids already integrated into society. They mingle with us socially and in the workplace. We see them on the streets, in grocery stores, in our neighborhoods, in schools, restaurants, hospitals...they are everywhere. It is imperative to acknowledge their presence. This is not a new situation, they have been here for millennia, although the number of off-planet beings is increasing exponentially. We must continue to speak out concerning our individual experiences although caution should be exercised since there is always a risk of job loss, estrangement with family and friends, and occasional government harassment to those who dare speak the truth. This gradually lessens individually and collectively as we continue to speak out, and more and more people are voicing acceptance of alien contact. It is wise to choose venues where it is safe, as these are the places where it will be most effective. We must continue encouraging our elected representatives to conduct hearings wherein we are allowed to tell of our experiences without fear of retribution.

Those of us privileged to be guests on world-wide talk shows are in the forefront of the Galactic Diplomacy advocacy. We speak to millions of people daily, providing listeners with the courage they need to share their experiences of contact and abduction. Those of us who write books on the subject also offer silent courage to those previously too timid to speak out. What will people say? What will they think? What might they do? These are legitimate fears that prevent people from confessing that they have been abducted, or voicing the suspicion that they may have an alien child.

We must put aside our fears to speak out and then stand our ground once we have done so. The truth is that once a person acknowledges interaction with a hybrid or an alien, the only consequences are the experience of a tremendous load having been lifted from their shoulders, and the power and knowledge that they are free to explore the new world that has been shown to them.

In *The Indigo Children*, Mr. Carroll and Ms. Tober define the phenomenon. *Indigos*, they write, share traits like high I.Q., acute intuition, self-confidence, resistance to authority and disruptive tendencies, which are often diagnosed as attention-deficit disorder, known as A.D.D., or attention-deficit hyperactivity disorder, or A.D.H.D. Offered as a guide for "the parents of unusually bright and active children," the book includes common criticisms of today's child rearing: that children are overmedicated; that schools are not creative environments, especially for bright students; and that children need more time and attention from their parents. But the book seeks answers to mainstream parental concerns about the paranormal.

In 2006, I made a real effort to cover more contactee cases and I began by flying to Lincolnshire, England to the home of Jason Andrews. The book *Jason;, My Indigo Child* was written by Ann Andrews and her son Jason. I was greeted by Paul and Ann Andrews and Jason and his wife Jacqui who live nearby in their own apartment. The Andrews house is located on two powerful lay-lines and is filled with paranormal phenomena. This includes entities, ghostly figures, UFO sightings and dimensional shifting and all those other situations that Ann Andrews recounts in detail in her book. I can attest to the fact that these things are true because as I was a guest in their home for the first three nights, but I asked to go to a motel the last three nights. The second night there I heard my name clearly called by a man with a British accent in the room where I was sleeping, Jason's old room. The third night, I took some photos of unusual phenomena in the hall where the staircase was. I heard footsteps all night long of someone walking up and down the stairs. Ann and Paul Andrews are used to this and it does not disturb them. But they have had twenty some years of someone taking their son and their finding him in odd places, twenty years of ghostly people in their yard and twenty years of being watched by ETS. To give the reader a better insight into what Jason is all about, I have included parts transcript of an interview that he agreed to do some time ago for the *Discovery Channel.*

"Question: It has been well documented now that you possess certain abilities, which are unusual to say the least! You claim that you have endured abductions by alien beings for most of your life but you are now at a point in your life where you both welcome their intrusion and actually learn from them. You even go as far as to state that 'they' have awakened you to the reality that you yourself are of alien origins. As 'they' have taught you so much, could you explain perhaps, how you are able to travel astrally and astrally project yourself?

Jason: These two are not the same thing; they are different. To astrally project myself to another place, I simply concentrate and think hard that I want to see that place; all of that place; I want to be there in the same reality in which I exist here. To be able to see and be seen. Part of me; myself; my energy then goes to that place and sends images to my brain. I can even communicate with people whilst there and again my brain is able to store the conversation as if I had physically been present. Obviously, as most of my energies are still here within the physical, I suppose I must seem like an apparition; a ghost or something whilst I'm there, but I can still walk around and talk in this reality. It's a bit like watching a television program whilst doing loads of other stuff at the same time. Astral travel is much easier and most people can do it – whether conscious of being able to do this or not. It happens when you are out of body. You are able to move easily and freely through objects, through walls, etc., and just wander around in that state. The more you are able to master this, the faster you are able to move and can take yourself anywhere. As you don't have to worry about breathing or drowning or anything, you can go anywhere – even space."

When asked about the knowledge he was given, Jason answers citing *the Source.* I realized that Jason is very wise for his age and he could be speaking here about some of the principles I discussed in this book about the cybernetic entities called the *Council of Nine* or the *Nine.*

Although he may not be referring to them specifically, the concept of the *Source* or God is very interesting.

Jason answers like this; "Let me first say that no-one ever knows everything. That is for the *Source; the One.* And you're wrong because it isn't a case of knowing; of having immense knowledge but the art is in knowing how to use that knowledge; having the key to it if you like. Know how to use the knowledge that you have and you will go far.

My understanding is that aeons ago there was the void and out of the void some sort of energy began to be. As this energy grew, it became powerful and, over time, the 'Source' split itself into other energies much like itself. There were twelve forms of energy to be exact. This is where your Bible gets confused. The scribes write about twelve disciples, twelve tribes of Israel, etc., They are really referring to the twelve entities if you like produced by the Source. These new forms dispersed throughout the void and gradually created the Universe. As the decades passed, their knowledge increased. So, technically, your 'big bang' theory would be correct in a way if you perceive that everything is energy and it reacts against itself. Of course, the more intelligent the twelve became, the more independent they were and, to my knowledge, three of them committed the ultimate sin and went against the Source by interfering with the creations they had helped to mould. As I said earlier, we can only advise and help whenever possible but we can never interfere directly. The consequences of their actions were that they were cast out from the Source (you know like your Bible says that God cast out the Devil). Doesn't mean that they were evil as such but you can't ignore the ultimate and only rule. The nine remaining have visited you from time to time throughout your history and you have known them as great men; like Jesus Christ, the Buddha, Allah, etc., but they've been to other places too throughout the Universe and have been acclaimed in much the same way. I do some healing in the physical sense when my parents allow visitors to come to the house and, as with all healing, it is all about moving the energies around in people's bodies and unblocking them. There are no guarantees but if the damage isn't long term, then I can usually help. In these circumstances, I like to try and teach the people who come for healing how to sort themselves out in the future and for most of them this has been very successful.

Jason speaks about *Indigo children* or star children from direct experience and I think that this helps the reader understand that there is a new generation being born that can easily navigate between two worlds and that they use telepathy. This is the generation that might indeed be able to communicate with an "orb" or an intelligent light being. Jason Andrews explains it like this;

"The 'Star Kids' are mostly born to parents where one of whom is an alien abductee – whether they are aware of this or not – but most parents do know. These children are incredibly bright even at a very young age and they know from the beginning that, whilst they love their parents, they understand that their real home is elsewhere – out there somewhere amongst the stars. This feeling often fills them with sadness; a longing to explore and discover just who they really are although they know that when they are ready, this information will be revealed to them – just as it was to me. They will find for the most part that they don't fit in with conventional society and its demands. As they grow, they feel almost limiting in their physical bodies as they know that they are so cumbersome and that they themselves are capable of so much more – but this has to be confirmed to them. I use the word confirmed as, like I said, these kids know exactly who they are – and more to the point, just why they are here at this precise moment in time. Ultimately, they are your salvation. They are the new race of humanity who, if allowed, will lead the World on its pathway to peace and understanding. These kids are now being recognized the world over. Dr. Richard Boylan in America is working with a lot of them. This is happening too in Australia and, to a lesser extent, in the United Kingdom too. A lot of these so called 'experts' are skeptical about their abilities – and their motives – whilst still other 'experts' put them under the supervision of psychiatrists 'for their own good

Protocol Seven

International Cooperation and Research Criteria

We need International cooperation. We need an International panel to create these Protocols.

This is about the planet Earth and not about any individual country.

We are one species: human

- Can we cooperate in good faith with our own colleagues on an International level to develop some scientific criteria for investigation?

- Serpo: Can we have a planetary exchange and has it happened already?

"I think the greatest lack in UFO research today is a lack of scientific methodology and rigor. Researchers should get together in a summit and decide on rules and protocol for separating good cases from those that are not. Also, it should be established what methods are best for investigating and discovering new knowledge from the good cases." Travis Walton (*OUR-J Magazine* Japan)

It is appropriate that I use this quote by Travis to lead into the protocols for investigation plus the protocols for the contact itself. Travis and Dana Walton have come to Rome twice and on one occasion stayed with me four days so I was able to talk to Travis on an informal basis. He is the same Travis as the one from 1975, incredibly honest and unaffected by his fame. After the incident he did not work in the forest very much. He worked for a number of years at a paper mill that manufactured wood trim and moldings. For the last three years, he has been working at a mill which makes paper from recycled paper material.

The thing that impressed me most was his ability to really reflect on his contact and look at it in perspective over so many years. In his questioning of the incident with possible government involvement, he says that " the *two blonde beings*" took him off the craft down a ramp into what could possibly be a government hanger. This brings up the *their stuff or our stuff* scenario I talked about earlier. He thinks there may be some governmental involvement since the hanger appeared to be a military hanger. Travis also says his case was not sufficiently investigated in a scientific way. He has a specific example of this. Travis claims that there was evidence that the tree growth in the forest was altered in the spot where the incident took place. By measuring the rings, the trees seemed to be growing 30% faster. Tragically this is a moot point now since most of the trees have burned down in a forest fire. We researchers waited thirty years too long to investigate this.

I also asked the obvious question, "What was the UFO doing there?" I asked about what was in the area. Dana, Travis' wife, told me that there had been some nuclear testing on the Nevada border nearby and some of the fallout was blamed for the rising cases of leukemia in bordering towns. She added there were quite a few court cases pending because of this. Is it possible "something" was monitoring the area? Is it possible that Travis reckless behavior by getting out of the truck interfered with this and the bolt of energy actually stopped his heart?

I was always wondering what the crystal-like devise was. It fell to the floor when he awoke so violently. Were they reviving him? Greys do not usually exit gracefully when one threatens them with a flashlight. There are anomalies in the case, anomalies that need to be studied. It may paint a more humane picture of the often, cruel scenario interpreted by abduction researchers. The protocols for contact cannot be applied to someone who is terrorized. Travis was totally terrorized and but in retrospect he may have acted differently.

It is interesting that when asked how he was transformed by this contact he says " before the incident I was open to the idea of UFOs and ETs because of sightings in years past by people I knew – and even myself. However, I had never seen anything that I could be completely certain was extraterrestrial. After the incident, I became more certain of the reality of UFOs and ETs" but he continues to say that some craft could possibly be ours. My experience was so traumatic that I still wish that it never happened but I have gained some very valuable knowledge about life and the universe.

If that incident was a demonstration of our technology, what were the two races of aliens doing there? If it was a hologram in 1975, what messages were given to the abductees including Travis? Who is promoting the "evil alien" scenario? All questions researchers should investigate. There always seems to be a nuclear involvement somehow. Both Einstein and Oppenheimer warned us about our dangerous nuclear involvement in the draft document of 1947. These are geopolitical concerns, as are the alien monitoring of our nuclear contamination of the planet. The nuclear question has been posed and intentionally ignored because most of us feel we can do nothing about it as we sit passively by as countries continue building weapons of mass destruction.

Is the Serpo story real? Did it happen?

Steven Spielberg's film *Close Encounters of the Third Kind* depicted 12 astronauts (some were women) who were selected to go with the aliens to their home world. Is this one of the foundations for *Operation Serpo* and is the alien exchange program a fabrication or was Spielberg shown the document by Reagan And he included it in his movie script? I cannot exclude that parts, if not the core of the film *Close Encounters of the Third Kind,* could be true. We need to consider the combination of disclosure "leaks" this year very curious. The release of the Robert Collins/ Richard Dody book *Exempt from Disclosure* in conjunction with the SERPO anonymous revelations makes one think. What is going on here? How much disinformation is mixed with this information? It is the dynamic team of Bill Ryan and Kerry Cassidy with their Whistleblower protection program that we need to watch. They are what a true investigative team should be, the true Mulder and Skully and perhaps, they have in hand the true *X-Files.* In a Laughlin interview with Bill Ryan, he counseled us all to examine carefully this story; to see that this could have been a logical progression to the contact of the Fifties and the government agreements made. For the open minded researcher, it is an opportunity to *connect more dots.*

Project Serpo is a term in ufology circles referring to an alleged exchange program between ultra top secret levels in the government of the United States and an alien home world called Serpo. It is speculated that Serpo is an (as yet officially uncharted) inhabited planet in the Zeta Reticuli system. Zeta Reticuli is a mapped binary star some 39 light years from Earth. In the 1990s, it was thought that a planet had been detected there by using advanced telescopes but that was later recanted by scientists who stated that it was merely a "wobble" caused by a pulsar. This has only increased speculation of a cover-up.(www.Sepro.com)

Bill Ryan, retired AFOSI Special Agent Richard Doty and author Whitley Strieber (writer of "Unknown Country") have all discussed Project Serpo. Project Serpo is an alleged secret exchange program of 12 military personnel to Serpo (and an unknown number of their kind to Earth) between the years 1965-1978. Ryan explained that he is a participant in a private ufology e-mail list moderated by Victor Martinez, and that in early November 2005. He receiving plausible messages from an "anonymous" contributor revealing information about Project

Serpo which Ryan has subsequently chronicled on his website. Bill Ryan reports on his website that there is said to exist a total of 3,000 pages of information on the project, which may be being released in installments – including transcripts (with original errors) of debriefing audiotapes possibly conducted under hypnosis. According to the "anonymous" source, Serpo is an Earth-sized planet with a population of around 650,000 alien beings (known in ufology as EBENs). An EBEN who allegedly survived the Roswell crash was said to have used a communication device to set up the exchange. Of the twelve who went on the exchange, eight returned (though all have since died), one died on Serpo, one died en route to the planet, and two remained there. Bill Ryan believes that the story has credibility and continues to provide us with up-dates.

Then in a timely manner, the book *Exempt from Disclosure* surfaced. The book title itself describes the status of classified information on UFOs. Veteran researcher, Robert Wood of the MJ-12 documents research reviewed this book and verifies some facts by saying:

"The record is unambiguous, powerful, and almost unarguable that there are many aspects of the UFO or flying saucer reports that have been classified over the years, and this is the first book that provides enough detail to convince many that we have had a deeply covert involvement with the UFO topic from the beginning. The two main authors, Robert M. Collins and Richard C. Doty, supported in part with documents provided by Tim Cooper, have painted what impresses this reviewer as an approximately accurate history of the handling of this topic inside the deepest confines of counterintelligence. Collins, a retired Air Force Intelligence Officer with the Foreign Technology Division, and Doty, a retired counterintelligence Air Force Office of Special Investigations agent, have put their knowledge together to create an impressively coherent history of the internal and external relationships surrounding the UFO topic in the United States. They identify specific people with seeming accuracy as to their involvement, and begin the story of their interaction in the fall of 1986. The book begins

with an appropriate chronology of the involvement with other interested (and usually "cleared") people, followed by the description of who has been involved with MJ-12 (the UFO management program) from the beginning, supported by photographs of those participating, many of whom are identified. More recent individuals that impressed this reviewer involved in MJ-12 as of 1986 included Senator Claiborne Pell, and Dr. Carl Sagan. Tim Cooper contributed direct quotes from his own father, an Air Force MSgt, who has high credibility supported by a certificate of commendation from General Le May for his "contribution to the Air Force UFO Program."

I also read the book and was impressed by the amount of information and names and places mentioned but distressed by the depth of the cover-up. The intelligence community enjoys seeing researchers " chasing their tails" in an effort to get to the *truth*, a truth that is hidden from us. But as the Honorable Paul Hellyer reminded me, that although shocking, *"the truth shall set us free"*.

Protocol Eight

Orbs, Spheres, and Intra-dimensional Beings

We need to find a way to communicate with orbs, spheres and intra-dimensional beings.

We need to find some common ground because they *do* exist.

- So where do we place orbs, and light beings in our mental data banks?

- What new cameras or technologies can be used to record them?

One review of Dr Lynne Kitei's documentary called *The Phoenix Lights* says "it is wide-ranging and insightful, with some original ideas thrown into the speculative mix. In the end, what is most striking about Kitei's coverage of the Phoenix Lights is the deeply spiritual significance that many of the people she interviewed ascribe to the phenomenon. Some declare that they have been irrevocably transformed by their sightings; their minds flung wide open by experiences that seem impossible to comprehend. Others find meaning and significance in the sense of peacefulness, awe, and wonder they experienced at the time of their encounters, recounting deep feelings of "appreciation for being alive and witnessing it." Since this is an *Orb phenomena* although many saw a boomerang craft, we need to consider the implications of these ETS showing themselves to Dr. Kitei and her family as well as hundreds of others in the city of Phoenix, Arizona Why?

Kitei herself, however, is surely the most profoundly affected, having committed much of her life to a passionate quest to understand her experiences. "Is humankind at large on the verge of understanding what experiencers of unexplained phenomena have known for millennia?" She writes in her book about the Phoenix Lights. "Are we now moving towards our next evolutionary level, the positive maturation and spiritual advancement of consciousness itself?"

Intelligent Light Beings can be extraterrestrial visitors. The Extraterrestrial visitors range from globes of light to small gray beings, to actual people who look like us. The extraterrestrial culture has grown around the presumed crash at Roswell, New Mexico in 1947 where a craft fell on the Brazel ranch supposedly brought down by the powerful radar that was used at the White Sands testing facility during the atomic bomb tests. The crash was cleaned up immediately Arm-Air Force and pieces taken to Wright Patterson Field in Ohio. It seems that six small grey bodies were recovered, one remaining alive and taken to the Nellis AFB Facility in Nevada which today is called Area 51. Over the years, many hundreds and thousands of people say they have had contact with extraterrestrial life. Swiss Farmer Billy Meier says that in the 70's he was visited by tall blond blue eyed Pleiadians which leads us to believe that the Cosmos is teaming with all types of Extraterrestrial visitors.

In his article *Mysterious phenomena are all around us, and within us,* Steve Hammons on October 30, 2005, says "Millions of people around the world are interested in "unconventional phenomena." These subjects include UFOs, crop circles, extra-sensory perception (ESP) and "remote viewing," near-death experiences (NDE) and life-after-death concepts and similar kinds of topics. In some cases, modern science is starting to understand many of these phenomena. Emerging understanding of physics explains the possible operation of some of these things. They may just reflect how the universe works, how Nature works. Even our military and intelligence communities have investigated these subjects.

The Army, CIA and Defense Intelligence Agency (DIA) have been involved in ESP and remote viewing for decades."

Ball Of Light Phenomena in Italy

BOL (*ball of light*)
**From Adriano Forgione, Editor
and owner Hera Edizioni
and Area 51 Magazines:**

Here is some starling new information from the field research I did on 26 June 2005, on the crop formation which actually appeared on 24 June 2005, in Montegranaro (Ascoli Piceno), Italy.

Before I left the formation at 9 p.m., after two hours of research on the Montegranaro site with Major, Mr. Gianni Basso, I took a last photo with the digital camera belonging to my friend, Ufologist Pino Morelli.

Recently, while scanning my archive, I was surprised to see a yellow-blue glowing light in the picture, behind my shoulders. I did not notice it in the darkness that night. However, it seems to be eight to ten meters away from me. There was nothing there, no houses, no streets or passages, only the rest of the field and some trees. Nobody else noticed the presence of the BOL (Ball of light) at that moment. I have made an enlargement of the BOL. (I attached to the photo section of this book.).

In the color version, there is a glowing, yellow-red corona around it, confirming the anomalous origin and the high temperature of the object, in complete accordance with the usual eyewitness testimony. I am sure it is not the result of the humidity and water in the air.

The incredible thing is that, right in the center of a soft cyan color BOL, there are the features of a *child's face*, "which seems to look at us (me in particular). I don't think this is an illusion. The features of this BOL are exactly the face of a child with an expression of surprise. It is the first time we have seen a BOL that looks like this. We find it incredible.

© Adriano Forgione – Pino Morelli. e-mail <u>adrianoforgione@ed izionihera.com</u>

Protocol Nine

Galactic Diplomacy and Cseti Protocols

It is important to establish who is in charge of formal *contact*. It must be done on a planetary level.

- The uniting of the world governments

- Choosing the "spokespeople"

- Some protocols like Cseti protocols are already in place

President Ronald Reagan first disclosed his recurrent thoughts about "an alien threat" during a December 4, 1985, speech at the Fallston High School in Maryland, where he spoke about his first summit with General Secretary Gorbachev in Geneva. According to a White House transcript, Reagan remarked that during his 5-hour private discussions with Gorbachev, he told [Gorbachev] to think, "how easy his task and mine might be in these meetings that we held if suddenly there was a threat to this world from some other species from another planet outside in the universe. We'd forget all the little local differences that we have between our countries "unfortunately with the wars and discords on Earth, it would take this scenario to unite the planet.

But there are those who do not agree as they see the alien presence as " benevolent" and "beneficial". It is Dr Steven Greer who developed the Cseti protocols for contact and so far has been the most respectful earthly ambassador. Founder of the Disclosure Project, Dr Steven Greer, shared secretive information about the Et presence, which, he said, has come to him from corroborated sources. One of his associates, who worked with Neil Armstrong at Purdue, said that Armstrong told him [that] once they stepped out of the lunar module on the Moon; they were literally surrounded by ET vehicles. Further, Armstrong was approached to be part of the Disclosure Project in 1997, but decline, over threats that his family would be killed, said Greer, who commented that fear and intimidation have kept many witnesses from coming forward. But how do we successfully integrate Cosmic Cultures into our current society?

It is interesting that in the *Einstein/ Oppenheimer document*, this statement appears.

"Now we come to the problem of determining what to do if the inhabitants of celestial bodies or (EBE) desire to settle here. They mentions if they are politically organized and possess a culture similar to our own, then they should be recognized as an independent people.

I believe that this is only respectful. What is interesting is that they suggest that a superior form of colonization would have to be conceived if we as a planet do not have political unity and we don't. This superior form of colonization would come about with the " *tacit approval* " of the United Nations. Here the United Nations is seen by the *Einstein Oppenheimer document* as a one- world government similar to what Dr. Mitchell suggested was needed for communication. The suggestion is made by Einstein- Oppenheimer that the United Nations become a "Supra-national" organization and vote to represent the nations of Earth in this Negotiation.

Ambassadors to the Universe Program: Protocols for Contact.

Exclusive Interview with Dr Steven Greer – Crestone, Colorado – July 4, 2005
www.DisclosureProject.org
www.CSETI.org.

Paola: Steven, what is the focus of your career at the present time?

Dr Greer: My main focus is still the CSETI encounters that we are doing now like this one at Crestone, Colorado. But there are different levels of this. We have people who train people like Dr. Loder and his people. There are others that get a group together and take them out in smaller groups, and have done 20 or 30 of these expeditions. They know what they are doing. The big trainings like this of 20 or 30 people I do. The main ones are Mt Shasta, Crestone and Joshua Tree Wilderness Area in California. The core basis of our focus is the fact that humans are going to have to learn to contact these non-human beings in a peaceful way and right now there is no initiative in the world that are doing this but ours. There are a few in Latin America that sort of have the same concept. Unfortunately the political structures have not dealt with the issue and the covert programs are military and hardly diplomatic. I mean they are actually increasingly hostile. What we are doing is a citizen's diplomacy effort and we have laid down protocols that are interrelated with very spiritually based and we believe that we are spiritually conscious beings and there is that one mind of the cosmos that shines in every being. This is the fundamental basis for help-ing to make contact and. because extraterrestrial technologies interface with thought and interface with what some people call the etheric or astral level of things, we have found that we can put together protocols that involve electromagnetic things like lasers and BP signals using this concept of sort of the center of the universal mind. In that center, we begin to see in sort of a remote sensing where the ETs are and connect with them mentally. We have had amazing contact, sightings and even things have come right to the field and what have you all over the world. So the concept is an very adapt one because it integrates the mind, the physical.

Paola: This is a very spiritual place here in Crestone. It has an incredible energy. There are many religions represented in this valley. I saw a Zen center and an ashram, and a center of Carmelite nuns.

Dr. Greer. There is a beautiful white stupa with the gold on top authorized by the Dalai Lama

Paola: Yes I saw that.

Dr. Greer: Yes. Ambassador Jim George from Canada was involved and was asked to build the stupa here and he did it. He is an advisor to our group and has spoken to Canadian officials about the energy problem and alternative energies. I just spoke in Montreal and there were over a thousand people there. I also spoke at the University of Toronto.

Paola: So Is the focus of your ET communication training a type of *Universal Cosmic Consciousness*?

Dr. Greer: Yes. You see the fundamental basis of being an ambassador to non-humans life forms, as I see it, is the understanding what it is, what's the Nexus where we all have some point in common. Well, it is not going to be that we are human with those who are non-human. So it is that we are conscious. And so, I remember Monsignor Balducci saying "we are all children of God" but there is this light of *Conscious Mind*, this one spirit within us all. There is *One Spirit* shinning through all of us, so by relating to that which, I feel is very important. I train people to do is take people to higher states of consciousness. I am taking people who are ready for that to a cosmic consciousness development retreat in Palm Springs in November. We will use meditation techniques and the contact techniques to be able to center and experience *Cosmic Mind* and then remotely view, using *Cosmic Mind*. We don't use the military system. It is very primitive. If we understand that the mind is omni-present. It is a singularity and we can settle into that "non-local" or expanded reality. You can see everywhere. People come on these retreats who have spent big bucks trying remote viewing and get these breakthroughs in three or four days because I am teaching them to stop and be still, and center and then use some specific techniques that I have learned to be able to remotely sense places and distant different objects. This training is very rigorous. And I think that people have to understand that the fundamental reason why that is important is that if you don't connect or relate to that aspect of *Universal Mind*, then how are you going to relate to non-human people? It doesn't make any sense. Think about it. They are not going to have the same emotional quality; they are not going to have the same mental aptitude; they are not going to have the same fountain of knowledge. They are not going to be biologically the same. So where are you connected? It is in this " conscious mind" which is the spirit! So in this kind of world, you not only have a diplomatic foundation for communication, but you also have a functional paradigm because their technology. It has been recorded at least in the 40's and 50's if not longer, they have devices that are electronic that interface with thought. They are not communicating with stellar systems in using microwave systems. They are using a sub-electromagnetic signal that interfaces with what the mystics used to call astral or thought energy and it is scientific reproducible. We have covert programs in the United States that develop these systems as well.

Paola: Edgar Mitchell used *thought transfer* from the moon and it worked!

Dr. Greer. Right, it does work. He and I talked about this. Every human being is a quantum hologram of the whole universe. In other words, I love this Sufi saying: "think yourself a puny form when within yourself the Universe is folded?" It is a rhetorical question. You are not a small thing. Within each person the entirety of the cosmic universe is unfolded literally. And opening to that you cannot only communicate with these extraterrestrial life forms but you can also begin to relate to a universal aspect of yourself. So you don't have to react to xenophobically when you encounter the diversity of extraterrestrial life.

Paola: Right. We already have trouble with diversity here on Earth.

Dr. Greer: My God, we are blowing people apart. We are spending a trillion dollars a year in military spending. So if we are going to be talking about a serious effort to become ambassadors to these other civilizations that are obviously involved with earth and obviously concerned with what we are doing, then those ambassadors, in my mind, have to be knowledgeable about the universal component of conscious. So I find that as the fundamental foundation of being an interplanetary ambassador so that is how I train people. That is the basis of what we are doing. A lot of people say that is very far out but it is actually simple because if you don't have something that you are anchored to that is deeper than the human, animal, intellectual emotional state, then you are not going to relate.

First of all, you can barely relate to another human from

another culture. Look how different an Italian is to a Japanese? You are talking about different star systems and people, and so to be able to transcend that level of diversity, and the diversity is fine if you are able to keep that perspective. But what happens is that you get overwhelmed by the diversity or that becomes a cause of conflict which is what human beings normally do. You know someone looks different, thinks differently. If they are gay, they are straight; they are black, they are white; they are Arab, they are Iraqi; they are Suni, they are Shiite; they are Protestant, they are Catholic; whatever it is we find a reason to blow each other apart. Well, we cannot export that kind of thinking to the next stage of human development which is the cosmic moment. This is a cosmic moment. The death throws of what is happening on Earth today is that this diversity is becoming a cause for conflict. It is really a spiritual problem as I see it. Now, I am not a religious person at all, but I am a spiritual person.

Paola: But you are optimistic, right? You could get real pessimistic if you look at the reality of this. You *are* developing an alternative.

Dr. Greer: Very optimistic. The whole thing is I think that we have to create a world that is commiserate with the challenges of our time and we have failed to do that. In other words, we are 100 or 150 years into this chapter of human history and yet we have refused to make the fundamental changes spiritually, socially, politically, geopolitically and technologically that would support a civilization commensurate with this time. For instance, we know that there have been technologies that could have eliminated world poverty and pollution that could have been here for 75 years. They went *deep black in* the 50's. The reality is that the human situation has been in a sense, retarded from an evolutionary developmental point of view for at least 50 to

100 years and this is why we see so much imbalance today. I'm optimistic that it will be brought back. But it is going to take courage, good leadership, some sacrifice which we had to face in our group. It is going to take some thinking in how we are going to create a civilization that is commensurate with the challenges of the time. There are many power dynamics working in this dysfunctional world that need to be fixed.

Paola: You articulate that really well, Steven. You are one of the only people who has put it together. I mean you synthesize this problem well. People have little pieces of it. Scientists are talking about *zero* energy and trying to figure out the propulsion systems. They do not look at the spiritual; they don't even talk about ET communication. Forget that! You synthesized the whole entire planetary situation and offered a possible solution in the *CSETI Ambassador Program of Consciousness*. You said you were working on three things. What are they?

Dr Greer: CSETI, the Ambassadors to the Universe program, the other is Disclosure Project. We are still doing the Disclosure Project because we have a website with ten million people on it. People don't realize that the Disclosure Project video has been seen by more people, than see CNN every night. I am still meeting with members of Congress. Within the last year, I'm trying to say "look this information exists and it is not only related to UFOs and extraterrestrials and but also to alternative energies and propulsion systems that would solve most of our problems. And so Disclosure still has to go on and we have a Disclosure some of the new top secret witnesses we have, and government officials including a former Clinton administration official. Also in technology where we can bring in scientists who can testify to the existence of new energy and propulsion systems, and how they have been systematically acquired and suppressed by large trans-national corporate interests representative's program. We also have dozens of people all over the world who host Disclosure Project screenings and meetings. So that is still going on. We would love to do Disclosure II. Many have yet to understand that after we did the *Disclosure Project* event in 2001, we doubled the number of military assets in terms of the number of witnesses because they came out of the closet. As a matter of fact, a retired Air Force general who has knowledge of these covert programs is one of them. The problem is that we do not have the funding to do it. We have got to find a source of institutional support and funding to be able to do the next level of it, or it is impossible to carry forward. There is no funding for anything serious and this is the whole tragedy of this effort. They just don't know what to make of it. You've got to connect it to something meaningful. The fact is that it is meaningful because there are enormous implications to the secrecy, and the secrecy is not because of the extraterrestrial component. The secrecy in the world UFO movement is because of the technology that would make obsolete all the oil and gas and coal power. It has become a carnival and caricature of itself, yet we are dealing with incredibly important things and my understanding is that the intelligence community which really does run the UFO subculture, wants to keep it that way. Now what I'd like to do in the next year or two is do another level of disclosure where we would bring in more witnesses. Most people post 9-11 really don't care if there are UFOs and ETs out there. But the majority of Americans do believe UFOs are real. Former CIA Director, William Colby, had an ET energy device that he was going to share with the *Disclosure* group, but just before he was going to do this, his body was found drowned off the Potomac. So secrecy is taking its toll and I believe it is time for *full disclosure*.

Steven Greer and I strongly agree with the words of the honorable Paul Hellyer stated in Kona Hawaii in June 2006.

"Evidence indicates that the survival of the planet as a reasonably friendly and hospitable environment is at stake, and that vested interests may be blocking plans to save it before it is too late. Even worse, the Military Industrial Complex is creating and producing weapons systems designed to confront visitors from space and, in the process, is proceeding to a situation which could be a sure-fire recipe for a possible conflict. One hesitates to contemplate the unknown and potentially disastrous consequences. Only an early and complete disclosure of the truth can save us from our folly."

Let's Change the Prime Directive
"The Agony and the Ecstasy of Ufology: The Emergence of Exopolitics and Galactic Diplomacy as Academic Disciplines."

By Paola Leopizzi Harris

In the these days when the fate of the planet is hanging by a thread in the Middle East and thousands of innocent civilians find themselves caught in the ideological political struggles of the major powers on the planet, *someone* is watching.

We, who have been following the phenomena since the 1947 Roswell crash during the testing of the atomic bomb at White Sands Proving Grounds, knew *someone* was watching then as *someone* is watching now. Those who were in the Pacific campaign during the second world war knew *someone* was watching especially close to the Island of Titinian while the French were doing nuclear testing off the Hao Reef from 1966-1969, the military knew they were also being watched. Witness testimony from geo-physicist Guy Andronik tells us he saw two different fly-overs of UFOs during that time. In an interview, Andronik told me he was present when they scrambled a plane to follow "the intruders." All this says that they must have been *the watchers* who have a prime directive: *Non interference with a primitive species during their evolutionary period.* Looking at this scenario, I believe we have come to a crossroads not only of aggression and war but also of a certain insensitivity to the evidence of Extraterrestrial visitations. Audiences still listen to speakers at conferences but then go home, have a few beers and switch on the game. There seems to be a de-sensitization of this phenomena by our very lifestyle. Recently a close girl friend of mine put it aptly when she said "I do not want to know if there are UFOs; I have enough to worry about"! This reminded me of a very discouraging statement made by aeronautics heir John Lear whose father developed the Lear Jet. In a recent interview, he commented on the disclosure efforts of serious researchers in this way.*"T'was a noble effort by noble people. Unfortunately they had not the slightest idea of the ramifications of what they were trying to disclose. In their naive innocence, they assumed they were disclosing the existence of flying saucers from outer space. What they failed to realize is that not everybody is ready for that information. Probably 99 and 99/100% are not. That information would not help them in their daily lives. It would not help them raise their children. It would not help them pay their taxes. It would not provide them with more income. It would not provide them with a new God. As a matter of fact it might destroy their faith in their old God. Those for disclosure only want one thing: they want to prove THEY KNOW THE TRUTH ABOUT FLYING SAUCERS. So do a lot of other people. Get over it. Its an ego trip. Let go. It's not time and won't be time for several generations. Relax, disclosure is none of your business. Have a sip Courvoisier XO and a Cohiba Esplendido and talk about it amongst your friends but don't try to go on Larry King and bang the U.S. Government over the head with a flying saucer. They don't know what's going on either. Have a heart."*

He is absolutely correct! This is the pathetic state of affairs on planet

Earth in 2006. So some researchers may say "why bother"? To add to this negative picture, a famous radio host recently commented while about Buzz Aldrin's denial of his sighting UfOs during the Apollo 11 Moon Mission, and he said "again we do not have a shred of *real evidence* after all this time that proves the existence of UFOs. May I remind him that just because someone of the caliber of Buzz Aldrin denies it, it does not mean other astronauts deny it. To add insult to injury, Buzz Aldrin in that same radio interview used the old " speed of light argument" to explain why ET can not come here. With discoveries in cutting edge quantum mechanics, we now know that no one in their right mind accepts this argument anymore. This statement sets us back eons. Is it true that we are no further along in acquiring proof after Buzz Aldrin cautiously denied he saw UFOs on the moon? Of course no one wants to explain the several film canisters which are actually missing from the NASA moon footage in the National Archives. Only Richard Hoagland does.

On his website *www.enterprisemission.com,* Richard Hoagland is addressing this mystery showing real Apollo 11 Moon Mission photographs. Thank God! In 2006, Richard Hoagland, Steven Greer, Ryan Wood, Bill Hamilton are still plugging away even after the negative Lear statement. But is it worth all this effort and money that we researchers put into disclosure when the result is total apathy? Maybe it is a problem only in United States. I can only write about what I witnessed this year.

On July 22rd 2006, MUFON researcher Alejandro Rojas, passionately orchestrated "Colorado Briefing" on the grounds of the State Capital in Denver, Colorado. Inside the beautiful Greek amphitheater, David Sereda, documentary film maker from California spoke of his film *Dan Akroyd- Unplugged,* Leo Sprinkle, senior professor and abduction Researcher from the University of Wyoming, spoke about current abduction research and Ryan Wood spoke about his new book *Majic Eyes Only.* Wood explained that there were at least 70 crashes after

Roswell documented in his book. Denver policeman Ken Storch spoke about Dr J.Allen Hynek, the Lonnie Zamora case and of his very own sighting of a UFO over Colorado. Lastly, I spoke about the signing of the ET Citizen Diplomacy document called the **Hawaii Declaration** by former Minister of Defense Paul Hellyer and US Ambassador John McDonald and many top researchers..

We were a formidable cast of credible speakers briefing the Colorado Public on the Denver Capital grounds. But maybe John Lear is right. No one really cares. I must admit there was little media attention with approximately 30 people seated in the hot sun while perhaps the rest at home prefer "not to worry about UFOs". We may refer to that as " the agony" of the many disclosure efforts. But still overhead *someone* is watching!

On the other hand, there is ecstasy in this work. Disclosure goes on in the highest level. Jesse Marcel Jr. was just of 11 years old when he saw and handled the Roswell debris. He says his dad woke his family up at 3:00 am in the morning spread some of the debris out on the kitchen floor to show it to them. Ironically, in a recent interview, Jesse Marcel Jr. told me he currently in the military and just returned from Iraq. Does he care about disclosure? He said *"I'd like people to know we are not alone in the Universe. These beings may have survived their nuclear conflicts but I am not sure we will"*.

He just wrote his account of Roswell in a new book called *Roswell: It Really Happened*. On the other side of the same coin is Edgar Mitchell's testimony. It was a pleasure but no surprise when I heard Edgar Mitchell, in San Francisco on June 7th 2006 at the Institute of Noetic Sciences' lecture, when asked if he believed in UFOs, answer in this way: *"I have never had doubts that of the millions of planets and galaxies out there, that there is life. Yes! I believe in UFOs but I had no personal first hand experiences except that I have been briefed by people "in- the-know", high level superiors, and old timers who had these particular jobs in Intelligence. They were there especially during the Roswell event and others since then and they had no doubt in their minds because they were there first hand. In addition to that, I had an opportunity to go to the Pentagon with these questions and then to a man in high level position of intelligence and I told him what I thought; what I heard. He did not know, but he said if that is true he should know and he will investigate..* Mitchell continued *"people know I am on the Board of NIDS (National Institute of Discovery Science) and I have seen that there are events that are very strange and could be ET related. Certainly we know that the Soviets have had these encounters and have had their Air Force chase them down, unsuccessfully of course. Also the French have put out the "Cometa Report" where high level officers told of their experience and asked their government to take it seriously. Two years ago Belgium made their knowledge official and then there are still the reports out of Mexico. So the answer is "yes"! There is a cover-up."*

Mitchell added *"You want to know why it has been covered up? That story is not too hard to explain. It goes to the mid 40's the Roswell incident was 1947. At that time President Truman was taking over from Roosevelt. The Army Air Corps became the US Air Force. The OSS had been disbanded and CIA came on board instead. It was not quite sure that anybody knew " who was on first". When the Roswell incident took place, a number of people, whom I knew, including Werner Van Braun, were called there to investigate this. A committee of high level people was set up by Truman. It was a committee called the Military Joint Intelligence committee and there were 12 individuals so the abbreviation MAJIC was the name of this organization. Although the name has changed over and over again, that committee still exists. That is one of the things my contact confirmed. There was a Executive National Security law that was passed and unthinkingly, it was given such power over years that they are accountable to no one. Even presidents at this point can't adequately have access. Other Presidents have tried but as far as I know Eisenhower and perhaps Kennedy was the last one to have full access."*

These words brought an applause. For me, it was one of those ecstatic moments where someone the caliber of Edgar Mitchell, Apollo

14 Astronaut who, like Buzz Aldrin, also walked on the moon, had the courage to address the UFO question publicly and ask for a certain openness.

Likewise, ex-minister of Defense, Paul Hellyer in Canada told me that we needed to know the "whole picture" before countries allocated huge amounts of money *to shoot aliens out of the skies*. He used the word *aliens!* We need to be grateful for these small steps in disclosure. They keep us researchers going.

Often, I am asked why I work in this field of information gathering and disclosure? I must admit, I am often discouraged. Although I do think often of the John Lear "who cares" response, I also remember the courageous ones; Dr. J Allen Hynek, Colonel Philip Corso and Dr. Michael Wolf Kruvante who are no longer with us. Like them, I believe the following:

1) Disclosure and the serious study of UFOs is a matter of National Security and we need to know who we are dealing with before we shoot. It is a political or rather an Exo-political concern to countries, especially to finance a "space war, perhaps the next war Werner Van Braun warned us about.

2) It is a fact that we are visited by different races, they could have a relationship to us as a human species. Could we be inseminated from the stars as most indigenous people believe?

3) These visitations are of ancient origins and we may need to rewrite our true history and update our archives. That will be essential for future generations.

These are three powerful arguments for continuing UFO research but this brings back to the precarious state of this planet currently at war. Besides having to worry about UFOs after viewing Al Gore's powerful film, *An Inconvenient Truth,* I realize we have ten years to worry about complete environmental destruction.

In San Francisco, Edgar Mitchell who also saw the film summed it up by saying this. *"The reality of this and the ET issue is that we have not been able to move government at any level in our country so other countries will move on it. I, frankly, believe we have far more serious issues right now than the ET presence. If these creatures are benign and there are conflicting stories, they may try to help us out. But it seems they are trying to take a "hands off, wait and see what happens attitude" to us!. Our major problem is sustainability, (survival) and the consumption ethic. All of these facets are about to be featured in brand new ways and Al Gore's environmental global warning is the beginning of it. I'm hoping that we will get all these issues, that are hidden and important to our way of life, opened up."*

So do I Dr. Mitchell. Let's hope *someone* is still watching because we may need to change the "Prime Directive" and actually ask for help from the Stars!

Possible Solutions

"We seek a free flow of information.. We are not afraid to entrust the American people with unpleasant facts, foreign ideas, alien philosophies, and competitive values. For a nation that is afraid to let its people judge the truth and falsehood in an open market is a nation that is afraid of its people.

John F. Kennedy

Solutions: "Establishing a new *"World View"*

Last interview with Dr. John Mack in November 2004 Florence, Italy

Paola: Thank you John for accepting the invitation by the very young group of GAUS students (Gruppo Academico Ufologico Scandici) to speak in Florence. Can you give us an overview of your career and your struggles in this arena. Can you give us your perspective of the abduction phenomena?

Dr. Mack: Sure I can give an overview of the "so called abduction phenomena and lead into questions of how do we know or what are the ways of knowing when we are dealing with something this strange. I can also will discuss the implications of this and phenomena like this for our world. I am a psychiatrist and psychoanalyst and I have a special interest in extraordinary experience.

Paola: Maybe you can also speak to language and how we perceive the world. I, personally, prefer the word "contact" rather than abduction because it seems a more positive.

Dr. Mack: This is true. For instance words like "abduction" and alien shape the conversation a certain way. The word "abduction" is off in two different ways. First, it implies that every person who has this encounter experience is taken against his or her will like an abduction in human terms. It also implies that each person who has an experience is physically taken, the whole body is taken up into a craft, which is also not true in all instances. Another aspect of contact is transferring information to humans telepathically or showing us images.

Paola: So are there particular reasons for this contact. What do your patients or "experiencers" say?

Dr.Mack: A lot of this information has had to do with what our species are doing that is destructive to our planet. It is as if what we are doing ecologically with the planet is creating some kind of larger problem in the Galaxy. Also" *the experiencers* "are given certain skills, certain capabilities that they were not given in their schooling. For instance they may discover that they may have a great artistic ability that comes from this contact. Also they may have been given important mathematical and scientific knowledge that goes way beyond anything they learned in school and yet they are downloaded the most complicated mathematical formulas and when the scientist and physicist recognize that there is truth coming from these individuals and sometimes more than the physicists themselves know, they recognize it as genuine. I have personally seen many examples of these.

Paola: The outside world always wants scientific evidence. What do you tell them?

Dr. Mack: About the question of evidence, how do we know that this experience is true? How do we evaluate these reports and how do we determine truthfulness. For example when I evaluate, I become clear that people of sound mind have no reason for making up this story. It is sure that they did not get it from the media because often they know more than the media. But there is something missing in what we have to evaluate or determine when a person tells us a story so bizarre whether he/she is telling the truth and whether we should take them seriously. But as yet we have had no criteria to evaluate the truth of such encounters. So I am working on just this and I'm just beginning to establish a science of human experience. Now in traditional science when we observe certain phenomenon, we bring some objectivity to what we have studied. But when you are trying to understand something so profound and important to a person you cannot stand back but you must enter "into "the consciousness of that person. So what the critics will say "what you are learning is too subjective". Here is the problem. If you are going to learn about something this profound, then the learning needs to be "intersubjuctive. " So still there is the problem of discovering the truth. If I say it just feels like they are telling the truth, then this is not enough. So we have to start with the "holistic way of knowing".

Paola: So how would you describe this way of knowing? Are these reliable witnesses?

Dr. Mack: Well, this is close to what we know as intuitive knowing. It is like a "knowing of the heart "and a "knowing of the spirit " that has been part of traditional cultures for hundreds and thousands of years but has been lost in the west. I received some help in this matter from Vatican Representative, Monsignor Corrado Balducci who says "we in the church take this UFO

Encounter Phenomena very seriously and the reason for that is, that there seem to be so many reliable witnesses. In the church, we have had centuries of having to evaluate miraculous reports by some kind of criteria and so they had to develop the notion of the "reliable witnesses." So I began to apply this idea of the reliable witness to these cases. How do we know who is a reliable witness? For my cases, it not only had to do with the fact just that these people who were trustworthy reported something but it had to do with the power of their communication that came across to me. I would experience with these people when they would be reliving their experience, the most powerful vibration. I was in the presence of something awesome in its intensity. The experiencers themselves would give language to that. They would say something like "every cell in my body was vibrating"! When you are in the presence of that, it passes your judging mind and you feel it in your whole being. Going back to "what is a reliable witness". It has to do with a resonance between the person who is reporting or sharing the experience and the clinician. It might be called "a direct knowing". You just know that with your whole being that this person is telling the truth. There are other examples of this "direct knowing" as demonstrated when the tribunal that was hearing testimony of the torture in Bosnia, and questioned witnesses. The judge said after hearing the testimony of a particular woman about how she was tortured." I do not need any more testimony". I can just tell that it is not possible that she is not telling the truth. That is sufficient. Now everyone knows torture exists. That is accepted. But it is not accepted in our society that these UFO encounters exist. Therefore you need to have evidence of a pattern of such similarities that is showing up in hundreds, if not, thousands of cases. One of these experiencers is helping me out with this statement she made about witnesses She said. "when a witness speaks, all recognize that they have been in another realm. Sincerity and truth and power of spirit are just as measurable as inches and pounds but not in the same way."

Paola: I think that it is the culture we live in who thinks all this is a "fringe" *New Age* subject. It is weirdness for them but you said once that not all cultures think this way.

Dr. Mack. True. It is ironic that experiences like alien abduction encounters, UFOs, crop circles, and near-death experiences are called anomalies. In another words, in our culture, what lies outside the realm of the cultural agreement about what is real is called anomalous. Therefore a huge amount of human experience is called anomalous when I have discussed this with Native Americans, and they say it is not an anomalous. We know about this. It is part of the human experience.

Paola: I have heard both you and Dr. Edgar Mitchell talk about changing our old paradigm but calling it a " new world-view". Can you describe this in what we might consider "exopolitical terms. We certainly need to do something on this planet.

Dr. Mack: About matter of a worldview and how it works. It has always been referred to as a paradigm and it has more of a scientific meaning. But I prefer to call it *world view* because it refers to something bigger. A world-view is the way we organize reality. It is the way we believe things work. In a way it is like an instrument of navigation. Our *world view* is what holds the human psyche together. What I came to realize with that Harvard committee was that I was threatening the scientific medical *world view* by which they were living.. What has been the dominant *world view* in our society could be called Neutonian-Carticianism or anthropocentric humanist. It is a world-view that puts the human being as top of the cosmic hierarchy of intelligence. The simplest term for this is, that which I call, *Scientific Materialism.* In this world-view, matter and energy is the primary reality and there is no larger intelligence in the cosmos. The principle method of study is objectivitive reality which separates the investigator from the matter that is being investigated. Now in recent years, this view, which has dominated our society, is failing. It is failing in every important element that the *world view* is supposed to serve. First there is a huge amount of phenomena, which it cannot explain nor deal with. There is no method of study for many things that we are talking about today. Secondly, it leads to terrible destructiveness because it treats the entire planet as simply physical resources to fight over by those who are the most powerful and most important countries.

Thirdly, "scientific materialism" does not give human beings any real satisfaction. It leaves us without spirit and it leaves us with an empty feeling. Because all it has to offer are more and more material things. Now we have new emerging *world views* that are different. In this *world view,* there is intelligence dwelling in the universe. That experience which happens to my clients is one example of the intelligence dwelling in the universe and the beings that have come to my clients are another example. The crop formations are also evidence of this intelligence that is trying to communicate with us. Also it is a model of the universe and us in it which says that everything is connected with everything else and we know that "cutting edge" physics is supporting this world-view. So it includes not only "new ways of knowing" but it also involves a spiritual awakening. This change which is happening around us is met with enmity and a great deal of resistance because there's a huge psychological economic and political investment in maintaining the old world-view. I will give you one examples of the UFO resistance because books being written which discuss this new paradigm are being called "new age, pseudo-scientific, pseudo-centric" in order to dismiss them as "out- of- hand" because some people who write such books do not hold themselves responsible to any scientific standards what-soever. I will conclude by speaking about the *implications* of this new *world view*. We see around us all kinds of forces which are supporting the emergence of this way of thinking. People around the planet are opening up to new ways of thinking. Groups, like the GAUS, these young people here in Florence, are committed to the new emerging paradigm. How would this planet be dif-ferent if the emerging *world view* became be the dominant *world view*? We would be connected to all living beings not just those around us, and with all nature and spirit which would make it impossible for us to treat nature in such a exploitative way. For example, we would be able to identify with other peoples, other religions and with all animals so we would not treat them just as products to consume. With this deeper reality, we could appre-ciate that we are connected to the Divine, the creative principle which would be more fulfilling than the material focus that has been so dominant today. So it would be global like a "global awakening of the heart" instead of global exploitation, a word that has that connotation today. I might add " the opening of the heart " has been a fundamental aspect of alien encounter experience. I learned this from my dealing with experiencers. Sometimes experiencers get information from these beings that we are not just a menace to the Earth but we are a menace to the Galaxy. In conclusion, as this emerging paradigm this emerg-ing *world view* takes hold, we might become more responsible citizens of a galaxy instead of becoming the eminent menace we appear to be!"

This was one of Dr. John Mack's last interviews and it was very powerful. This philosophy is somewhat sustained in the Einstein/

Oppenhiemer paper when they say " *It would be difficult to predict what the attitude of International law would be with regard to the occupation by celestial peoples of certain locations on our planet but the only thing that can be foreseen is that there will be a profound change in traditional concepts*".

Epilogue

So how does one speak to a *Ball Of Light*? Alien Communication; Light Spheres, Kyle XY, and Psychics Aliens among us?

Part of this book on Exopolitics book is called *"How does one speak to a ball of Light?* It is about exoplolitical challenges and protocols of future contact and among them communication with *alien entities*. It implies that one can not use ordinary human languages to communicate with all things *alien*. In this book, I speak of *intelligent light spheres* who interact with humans and I also speak about the mysterious light spheres that interact with electricity as seen in Caronia in Sicily where the houses seem to self combust without reason. However there seem to be no human causalities that we know of.

The irony is that I have received much criticism for the unconventional title of this book because we think of ET in terms of greys, Nordics and Reptilians. But there are also intelligent light forms, perhaps cybernetic beings. They are probably already here. They are probably among us.

The Use Of Telepathy

There are beings among us that range from *spheres of light* to those completely human. They pique our imagination and our curiosity. They are entering into the mainstream.

It is interesting how today people are ready to accept the TV series Kyle XY, a major hit on the American channel ABC. Seemingly an Alien or perhaps a "clone", Kyle has no belly button (umbellico) and sleeps in a bath tub. Kyle XY is a 16 year old boy with a mind of a genius. He's found wandering in the streets with no memory of who he is, or where he comes from. He is taken to a youth detention center where he meets Nicole Trager a psychologist who sees that Kyle has these amazing abilities. Not long before she wants to bring him home to her husband and two kids. While staying with the Trager family, Kyle starts to remember his past. Six episodes into its life, "Kyle" has become the most-watched original series ever on seen on ABC Family so far.. It draws about 2.1 million viewers per week, with close to 800,000 of those falling in the adults 18-49 demographic. Matt Dallas stars in the series as Kyle, who has a savant-like intellect but is as naive about the world as a newborn. The reaction of society is the non acceptance and persecution of anyone who is different and the problem is communication. You can not lie to Kyle XY because he uses mental telepathy. He can read your mind.

I found this is true of Savant clairvoyant 32 year old Pascal Riolo, Belgium's most successful psychic. It is not his readings for business or for private citizens, nor his spoon bending skills, nor his communication with other dimensions that impress me but his ability to communicate mentally; to see through you with his instant knowing. You cannot lie to Pascal. He can read your intentions.

I was the only journalist who in an interview asked how he acquired his abilities and he described a contact experience that reminds me of the light sphere that activated a 4 year old Uri Geller in a park in Tel Aviv, years ago. Instead this was Belgium, Pascal was five when, unexpectedly, he was separated from his parents at a picnic. He found himself on a beach on top of a cliff viewing the sea, despondent and afraid; so much so. that he considered throwing himself into the water. He recalls that he then heard a clear voice telling him not to do it. The voice said that he would be important for humanity and that he would help them. What was then quite amazing was that, out of nowhere a classmate arrived, a small boy like him who took him by the hand back to his parents. What was this voice and where did it come from and how did it communicate? This episode stays very vivid in Pascal's mind today as he considers this a beginning of his clairvoyant experiences. The use of telepathy or powers of the mind is easy for him and for Kyle XY and perhaps of "disembodied Intelligences" that interfere with the electrical system and self-combusting houses. But who is engaging *them* in this inter-dimensional dialogue?

Recently Stanford Research Institute Physicist, Russell Targ, was amazed when three quarters his audience, at a remote viewing conference in Rome, described the hidden slide correctly. Targ has written several books on remote viewing, consciousness and non-locality.

That audience was activated to believe that with constant practice they could hone their ESP Ability. People want to use this sixth sense but they do not realize two very important elements.

1) That if you allow many dimensional beings in your reality who have access to your thoughts they will read your mind so "You cannot lie."

2) That it could be very dangerous for the masses that constantly are faced with unethical decisions, immoral behavior and subjected to the powers who rule the Earth. This communication can border on could border on " mind control"

As the famous remote viewer, Ingo Swann, who collaborated with the United States Intelligence community said in his book *Penetration* "that the non-human intelligences were on the dark side of the moon." What is more interesting is he said that *they* were well aware of his presence. They knew he was watching *them* from Earth. This was obviously a two-way communication. So who or what is communicating from the moon?

Recently at a conference on Mj 12 Documents in Florence Italy, while special guest Ryan Wood spoke about the Roswell crash, two spheres of light, one intensely red and one pulsating white crisscrossed and darted around the room as a participant felt compelled to capture them on video from her cell phone. Is there a scientific explanation for these light spheres or is it a simple communication? Who knows? We should not rule anything out. So maybe there are intelligent balls of light or light beings who are so highly evolved that they can travel between dimensions. Thousands of orbs *with individual signatures* are now appearing and being photographed by our digital cameras, our cell phones and even our video equipment. What are they? I do not know but I know they are important signs. We need to leave an open mind to future possibilities of communication. It has become a relatively new study.

Can Cybernetic Brains exist devoid of bodies? Can we co-exist with Artificial Intelligence? Is Philip K Dick's vision of Valis the ultimate reality? Disembodied entities like " the council of nine" in Phyllis Schlemmer's book the *Only Planet of Choice* (Page 5) of this book, communicated with writer Gene Roddenberry (creator of Star Trek). He was told by an entity named Tom that *nine* is a complete number because it is whole and "*the nine*" are the aeons which is used to describe a period of time, an eternity. They describe themselves to Roddenberry as *the highest form of Celestial Power, spiritual disembodied entities formed from Divine Presence.* We know something inspired Roddenberry to create "Deep Space 9", the Star Trek sequel.

I believe it is becoming more mainstream to believe in mental communication and the power of telepathy. Television shows taken from real life like the ever popular "Medium" and the hit television series Kyle XY who live regular lives in mainstream society. Also increasing the popularity of "remote viewing" courses demonstrate that non-verbal communication, ESP and telepathy are a valid form of human communication with cosmic cultures and dimensional beings. They may be among us perhaps in a form of human aliens like Kyle XY or in some form of disembodied intelligences or *spheres of light* who want to communicate. They may be telling us something important as they dart around the room in Florence or atop a crop circle in England. They could be telling us this, as communicated in a transmission given to Phyllis Schlemmer for the book the only *The Planet of Choice.*

"We imbue you with energy. We awaken you, as you awaken us. We wish you to know we love you. We wish you to not make gods of us or of yourselves. We thank you"

The Hawaii Declaration

Hawaii Declaration on Peaceful Relations with Extraterrestrial Civilizations

We, the individuals and institutions participating in and/or supporting the Extraterrestrial Civilizations & World Peace Conference in Kailua-Kona, Hawaii, June 9-11, 2006,

Are a body of concerned private citizens who are promoting world peace and harmonious relations with extraterrestrial civilizations,

Recognizing the overwhelming evidence pointing to the presence of extraterrestrial civilizations, and their generally peaceful interaction with individuals and governmental authorities,

Inspired by the profound significance for humanity of sharing the wisdom, knowledge, culture and technology provided by extraterrestrial civilizations,

Asserting that extraterrestrial civilizations have been observing human evolution for some time with particular interest in humanity's quest for lasting peace among its peoples,

Noting that extraterrestrial civilizations have indicated that the abolishment of nuclear weapons worldwide is a necessary milestone toward peaceful coexistence on earth and as a prerequisite for open contact,

Recalling United Nations resolutions concerning international co-operation in the peaceful exploration and use of outer space, banning atmospheric and underwater nuclear tests, and proscribing hostile acts on the moon and other celestial bodies,

Recognizing a range of initiatives promoted by private citizens and citizen organizations with regard to extraterrestrial civilizations visiting Earth,

Intending for this Declaration to be used as a starting point for a greater public dialogue with those holding similar or diverging perspectives and interests concerning extraterrestrial visitation,

Using a consensual decision making process among speakers, organizers, and participants at the Extraterrestrial Civilizations and World Peace Conference, 2006, we have agreed to,

Honor the following principles for establishing peaceful relations with extraterrestrial civilizations:

1. We affirm the intent of humanity to join in peaceful and cooperative relations with extraterrestrial civilizations,

2. Affirm support for United Nations resolutions promoting the peaceful use of Outer Space, and support for UN, International and U.S. Congressional initiatives to prevent an arms race in outer space, including the weaponization of space,

3. Affirm the natural right of all citizens to have open contact with representatives of extraterrestrial civilizations in all cases, and to engage in non-official diplomacy,

4. Declare the need for Civil Society to develop acceptable protocols (standards of behavior) with extraterrestrial civilizations, that the protocols should be representative of the aspirations of all humanity, and that all nations should work in concert to establish peaceful relations,

5. Cooperate with extraterrestrial civilizations in promoting Earth, Cosmic and Life friendly technologies, and encouraging the right use and open availability of these technologies,

6. Affirm our desire to coordinate the earth's ecological health and biological diversity with extraterrestrial civilizations that can aid us in that endeavor,

7. And express our desire to welcome the open appearance of benevolent extraterrestrial civilizations.

***

Expressions of Support – Conference Organizers and Speakers

Michael E. Salla, PhD (Convenor/Speaker); Angelika Whitecliff (Co-Organizer); Hon Paul Hellyer (Speaker); Thomas Hansen, PhD (Speaker); Joan Ocean, M.Sc. (Speaker); Paola Harris, M.Ed. (Speaker); Alfred Webre, J.D. (Speaker); James Gilliland (Speaker); Robert Salas, (Capt USAF, ret.- speaker); Mary Rodwell, R.N. (Speaker); Neil Freer (Speaker); Scott Jones, PhD (Speaker); Philip Corso, Jr (Speaker); Darryl Anka (Speaker); Wendelle Stevens (Lt Col. USAF ret. – Speaker);

"A New World if you can take it" (Lt Col Philip Corso)

Official Conference website: www.etworldpeace.com

Declaration Online Petition:
http://www.petitiononline.com/ETPeace/petition.html

Conference Sponsor is the Exopolitics Institute:
www.exopoliticsinstitute.org

Kailua-Kona, Hawaii, June 11, 2006

Copyright © 2006 Exopolitics Institute

Author Biography

Paola Leopizzi Harris (Italy/Europe/Vatican) **www.paolaharris. com/**www.paolaharris.it is an Italo-American photojournalist and investigative reporter in the field of extraterrestrial related phenomena research. She is also a widely published, free-lance writer, especially in Europe. She has studied extraterrestrial related phenomena since 1979 and is on personal terms with many of the leading researchers in the field. From 1980-1986 she assisted Dr. J. Allen Hynek with his UFO investigations and has interviewed many top military witnesses concerning their involvement in the government truth embargo.

In 1997, Ms. Harris met and interviewed Col. Philip Corso in Roswell, New Mexico and became a personal friend and confidante. She was instrumental in having his book *The Day After Roswell*, for which she wrote the preface and it was translated into Italian. She consequently brought Colonel Corso to Italy for the editorial group Futuro, publisher of *Il Giorno Dopo Roswell*, and Corso was present for many TV appearances and two conferences. She returned to Roswell in the summer of 2003 for the American debut of her book, *Connecting the Dots; Making Sense of the UFO phenomena.*

Because of her international perspective on extraterrestrial related phenomena, Paola has consulted with many researchers about the best avenues for planetary disclosure with emphasis on the "big picture" and stressing the historical connection. She is a close friend of Monsignor Padre Corrado Balducci and assisted in filming the Italian witnesses, including the Monsignor, for the Disclosure Project for the May 9, 2001 press conference. She was instrumental in bringing to Italy Robert Dean, Dr. Steven Greer, Linda Moulton Howe, Dr. Richard Boylan, Russell Targ, Travis Walton, Derrell Sims, Helmut Lamner, Michael Lindemann, Nick Pope, Bill Hamilton, Ryan Wood, Carlos Diaz and Dr. John Mack. Her new non-profit association, Starworks Italia, will continue to bring speakers to Italy and promote disclosure and exo-political dialogue world-wide.

She has a regular column in Area 51 *UFO Magazine, has written for Nexus, Australia, Notizario UFO* and *Dossier Alieni,* among others publications.

Paola lives in Rome and Boulder, Colorado and has a Masters degree in Education. She teaches history and photojournalism and on-line classes in Exopolitics for Dr. Michael Salla's Exopolitics Institute for which she in International liason director.

Appendix and Bibliography

The 12th Planet
   Zecharia Sitchin

Alien Rapture
   Ed Fouche with Brad Steiger

And Still They Fly
   Guido Moosbruger

Briefings on the Future Landing on Planet Earth
   Stuart Holroyd

Behold a Pale Horse
   William Cooper

The Catchers of Heaven
   Dr. Michael Wolf

Close Extraterrestrial Encounters
   Dr. Richard Boylan

Cosmic Explorers
   Dr. Courtney Browne
   Cosmic Top Secret

Bill Hamilton
   The Day after Roswell
   Colonel Philip Corso

The Deepening Complexity of Crop Circles: Scientific Research & Urban Legends
   Eltjo Haselhoff

Destiny Matrix
    Dr. Jack Sarfatti

The End of Suffering
    Dr. Russell Targ and James J Hurtak

Exempt from Disclosure
    Robert Collins and Richard Doty

Exopolitics
    Dr. Michael Salla

Gene Roddenberry: The Last Conversation
    Yvonne Fern

Glimpses of Other Realities I and II
    Linda Moulton Howe

Hidden Truth; Forbidden Knowledge
    Dr Steven Greer

Jason; My Indigo Child
    Jason and Ann Andrews

Leap of Faith
    Gordon Cooper

Majiic Eyes Only
    Ryan Wood

Milabs
    Helmut Lammer

Millennial Hospitality
    Charles James Hall

Miracles of the Mind
    Dr. Russell Targ and Jane Katra

The Monuments of Mars
Richard Hoagland

The Only Planet Of Choice
Phyllis Schlemmer

Open Minds, Closed Skies
Nick Pope

The Path of the Explorer
Dr. Edgar Mitchell

Passport to the Cosmos
Dr. John Mack

Penetration: The Question of ET and Human Telepathy
Ingo Swann

Exopolitics: Politics, Government and Law in the Universe.
Alfred Webre

Project Aquarius
Bill Hamilton

Raechels's Eyes
Hellen Littrell and Jean Bilodeaux

*Soul Samples: Personal Exploration in Reincarnation and UFO
Experience*
Dr. Leo Sprinkle

The Stargate Conspiracy
Lyn Pickett & Clive Prince

The Terra Papers
Robert Morningsky

The UFO Experience
     Dr. J. Allen Hynek

UFOs Are Real
     Clifford Stone

Underground Bases and Tunnels
     Dr. Richard Sauder

Unorthodox Encounters
     Uri Geller

Uri
     Andrija Puharich

Witnessed
     Budd Hopkins

LaVergne, TN USA
06 December 2010
207546LV00001B/61/A